Cram101 Textbook Outlines to accompany:

Business Marketing Management

Michael D. Hutt, 10th Edition

A Cram101 Inc. publication (c) 2010.

PRACTICE EXAMS.

Get all of the self-teaching practice exams for each chapter of this textbook at **www.Cram101.com** and ace the tests. Here is an example:

Business Marketing Management
Michael D. Hutt, 10th Edition,
All Material Written and Prepared by Cram101

I WANT A BETTER GRADE.

1 _____ is the practice of individuals, or organizations, including commercial businesses, governments and institutions, facilitating the sale of their products or services to other companies or organizations that in turn resell them, use them as components in products or services they offer or use them to support their operations. Also known as industrial marketing, _____ is also called business-to-_____, or B2B marketing, for short. (Note that while marketing to government entities shares some of the same dynamics of organizational marketing, B2G Marketing is meaningfully different).

- ◯ Business marketing
- ◯ Baby monitor
- ◯ Back office
- ◯ Backorder

2 In mathematics, _____ and unDefined are used to explain whether or not expressions have meaningful, sensible, and unambiguous values. Whether an expression has a meaningful value depends on the context of the expression. For example the value of 4 − 5 is unDefined if a positive integer result is required.

- ◯ Defined
- ◯ Dabigatran
- ◯ Daewoo
- ◯ Daihatsu

3 _____ is a business discipline which is focused on the practical application of marketing techniques and the management of a firm"s marketing resources and activities. Marketing managers are often responsible for influencing the level, timing, and composition of customer demand accepted definition of the term. In part, this is because the role of a marketing manager can vary significantly based on a business" size, corporate culture, and industry context.

- ◯ Marketing management
- ◯ Maas International

You get a 50% discount for the online exams. Go to **Cram101.com**, click Sign Up at the top of the screen, and enter DK73DW10460 in the promo code box on the registration screen. Access to Cram101.com is $4.95 per month, cancel at any time.

With Cram101.com online, you also have access to extensive reference material.

You will nail those essays and papers. Here is an example from a Cram101 Biology text:

Visit **www.Cram101.com**, click Sign Up at the top of the screen, and enter DK73DW10460 in the promo code box on the registration screen. Access to www.Cram101.com is normally $9.95 per month, but because you have purchased this book, your access fee is only $4.95 per month, cancel at any time. Sign up and stop highlighting textbooks forever.

Learning System

Cram101 Textbook Outlines is a learning system. The notes in this book are the highlights of your textbook, you will never have to highlight a book again.

How to use this book. Take this book to class, it is your notebook for the lecture. The notes and highlights on the left hand side of the pages follow the outline and order of the textbook. All you have to do is follow along while your instructor presents the lecture. Circle the items emphasized in class and add other important information on the right side. With Cram101 Textbook Outlines you'll spend less time writing and more time listening. Learning becomes more efficient.

Cram101.com Online

Increase your studying efficiency by using Cram101.com's practice tests and online reference material. It is the perfect complement to Cram101 Textbook Outlines. Use self-teaching matching tests or simulate in-class testing with comprehensive multiple choice tests, or simply use Cram's true and false tests for quick review. Cram101.com even allows you to enter your in-class notes for an integrated studying format combining the textbook notes with your class notes.

Visit **www.Cram101.com**, click Sign Up at the top of the screen, and enter **DK73DW10460** in the promo code box on the registration screen. Access to www.Cram101.com is normally $9.95 per month, but because you have purchased this book, your access fee is only $4.95 per month. Sign up and stop highlighting textbooks forever.

Business Marketing Management
Michael D. Hutt, 10th

CONTENTS

Chapter 1. A Business Marketing Perspective

Business marketing	Business marketing is the practice of individuals, or organizations, including commercial businesses, governments and institutions, facilitating the sale of their products or services to other companies or organizations that in turn resell them, use them as components in products or services they offer or use them to support their operations. Also known as industrial marketing, Business marketing is also called business-to-Business marketing, or B2B marketing, for short. (Note that while marketing to government entities shares some of the same dynamics of organizational marketing, B2G Marketing is meaningfully different).
Defined	In mathematics, Defined and unDefined are used to explain whether or not expressions have meaningful, sensible, and unambiguous values. Whether an expression has a meaningful value depends on the context of the expression. For example the value of $4 - 5$ is unDefined if a positive integer result is required.
Marketing management	Marketing management is a business discipline which is focused on the practical application of marketing techniques and the management of a firm"s marketing resources and activities. Marketing managers are often responsible for influencing the level, timing, and composition of customer demand accepted definition of the term. In part, this is because the role of a marketing manager can vary significantly based on a business" size, corporate culture, and industry context.
Data migration	Data migration is the process of transferring data between storage types, formats, freeing up human resources from tedious tasks. It is required when organizations or individuals change computer systems or upgrade to new systems, or when systems merge (such as when the organizations that use them undergo a merger/takeover).
Consumer	Consumer is a broad label for any individuals or households that use goods and services generated within the economy. The concept of a Consumer is used in different contexts, so that the usage and significance of the term may vary. Typically when business people and economists talk of Consumers they are talking about person as Consumer, an aggregated commodity item with little individuality other than that expressed in the buy/not-buy decision.
Asset	In business and accounting, assets are economic resources owned by business or company. Anything tangible or intangible that one possesses, usually considered as applicable to the payment of one"s debts is considered an asset. Simplistically stated, assets are things of value that can be readily converted into cash (although cash itself is also considered an asset).
Market dominance	Market dominance is a measure of the strength of a brand, product, service, relative to competitive offerings. There is often a geographic element to the competitive landscape. In defining Market dominance, you must see to what extent a product, brand, or firm controls a product category in a given geographic area.
Marketing	

marketing is a "social and managerial process by which individuals and groups obtain what they need and want through creating and exchanging products and values with others." It is an integrated process through which companies create value for customers and build strong customer relationships in order to capture value from customers in return.

marketing is used to create the customer, to keep the customer and to satisfy the customer. With the customer as the focus of its activities, it can be concluded that marketing management is one of the major components of business management.

Xerox Corporation	Xerox Corporation is a global document management company which manufactures and sells a range of color and black-and-white printers, multifunction systems, photo copiers, digital production printing presses, and related consulting services and supplies. Xerox is headquartered in Norwalk, Connecticut , though its largest population of employees is based in and around Rochester, New York, the area in which the company was founded. The Xerox 914 was the first one-piece plain paper photocopier, and sold in the thousands.
	Xerox was founded in 1906 in Rochester, New York as "The Haloid Company", which originally manufactured photographic paper and equipment.
Proposition	This article is about the term proposition in logic and philosophy; for other uses see proposition
	In logic and philosophy, proposition refers to either (a) the "content" or "meaning" of a meaningful declarative sentence or (b) the pattern of symbols, marks, or sounds that make up a meaningful declarative sentence. Propositions in either case are intended to be truth-bearers, that is, they are either true or false.
	The existence of propositions in the former sense, as well as the existence of "meanings", is disputed by some philosophers.
Value	A personal and cultural value is a relative ethic value, an assumption upon which implementation can be extrapolated. A value system is a set of consistent values and measures that is soo not true. A principle value is a foundation upon which other values and measures of integrity are based.
Value proposition	In the field of marketing, a customer Value proposition consists of the sum total of benefits which a vendor promises that a customer will receive in return for the customer"s associated payment (or other value-transfer.)
	Put simply, the Value proposition is what the customer gets for his money.
	Accordingly, a customer can evaluate a company"s value-proposition on two broad dimensions with multiple subsets:
	· relative performance: what the customer gets from the vendor relative to a competitor"s offering; · price: which consists of the payment the customer makes to acquire the product or service; plus the access cost
	The vendor-company"s marketing and sales efforts offer a customer Value proposition; the vendor-company"s delivery and customer-service processes then fulfill that value-proposition.

A value-proposition can assist in a firm"s marketing strategy, and may guide a business to target a particular market segment.

Point

In typography, a point is the smallest unit of measure, being a subdivision of the larger pica. It is commonly abbreviated as pt. The traditional printer"s point, from the era of hot metal typesetting and presswork, varied between 0.18 and 0.4 mm depending on various definitions of the foot.

Today, the traditional point has been supplanted by the desktop publishing point (also called the PostScript point), which has been rounded to an even 72 points to the inch (1 point = $\frac{127}{360}$ mm ≈ 0.353 mm).

The demand

Perfectly inelastic demand Perfectly elastic demand

A price fall usually results in an increase in the quantity demanded by consumers . The demand for a good is relatively inelastic when the change in quantity demanded is less than change in price. Goods and services for which no substitutes exist are generally inelastic.

Parity

Parity is a concept of equality of status or functional equivalence. It has several different specific definitions.

· parity (physics), a symmetry property of physical quantities or processes under spatial inversion
· parity (mathematics), indicates whether a number is even or odd
· parity (medicine), the number of times a woman or female animal has given birth
· parity (charity), UK equal rights organisation
· parity (law), legal principle
· parity bit, sets the parity of transmitted data for the purpose of error detection
· Purchasing power parity, in economics, the exchange rate required to equalise the purchasing power of different currencies
· Interest rate parity, in finance, the notion that the differential in interest rates between two countries is equal to the differential between the forward exchange rate and the spot exchange rate
· Put-call parity, in financial mathematics, defines a relationship between the price of a European call option and a European put option
· parity (sports), an equal playing field for all participants, regardless of their economic circumstances
· Potty parity, equalization of waiting times for males and females in restroom queues
· A tactic in othello
· Grid parity of renewable energy "

Derived demand

Derived demand is a term in economics, where demand for one good or service occurs as a result of demand for another. This may occur as the former is a part of production of the second. For example, demand for coal leads to Derived demand for mining, as coal must be mined for coal to be consumed.

Monotonic function

In mathematics, a monotonic function (or monotone function) is a function which preserves the given order. This concept first arose in calculus, and was later generalized to the more abstract setting of order theory.

In calculus, a function f defined on a subset of the real numbers with real values is called monotonic (also monotonically increasing or non-decreasing), if for all x and y such that $x \leq y$ one has $f(x) \leq f(y)$, so f preserves the order .

Relationship marketing

Relationship marketing is a form of marketing developed from direct response marketing campaigns conducted in the 1970"s and 1980"s which emphasizes customer retention and satisfaction, rather than a dominant focus on "point of sale" transactions.

relationship marketing differs from other forms of marketing in that it recognizes the long term value to the firm of keeping customers, as opposed to direct or "Intrusion" marketing, which focuses upon acquisition of new clients by targeting majority demographics based upon prospective client lists.

relationship marketing refers to long-term and mutually beneficial arrangement wherein both buyer and seller focus on value enhancement through the certain of more satisfying exchange.This approach attempts to transcend the simple purchase exchange process with customer to make more meaningful and richer contact by providing a more holistic, personalized purchase, and use orn consumption experience to create stronger ties.

Supply chain

A Supply chain or logistics network is the system of organizations, people, technology, activities, information and resources involved in moving a product or service from supplier to customer. Supply chain activities transform natural resources, raw materials and components into a finished product that is delivered to the end customer. In sophisticated Supply chain systems, used products may re-enter the Supply chain at any point where residual value is recyclable.

Toyota

Toyota Motor Corporation is a multinational corporation headquartered in Japan, and currently the world"s largest automaker. Toyota employs approximately 316,000 people around the world.

In 1934, while still a department of Toyota Industries, it created its first product Type A engine and in 1936 its first passenger car the Toyota AA.

Best practice

A best practice is a technique, method, process, activity, incentive or reward that is believed to be more effective at delivering a particular outcome than any other technique, method, process, etc. The idea is that with proper processes, checks, and testing, a desired outcome can be delivered with fewer problems and unforeseen complications. best practices can also be defined as the most efficient (least amount of effort) and effective (best results) way of accomplishing a task, based on repeatable procedures that have proven themselves over time for large numbers of people.

Relationship management

Customer Relationship management (C Relationship management) consists of the processes a company uses to track and organize its contacts with its current and prospective customers. C Relationship management software is used to support these processes; information about customers and customer interactions can be entered, stored and accessed by employees in different company departments. Typical C Relationship management goals are to improve services provided to customers, and to use customer contact information for targeted marketing.

Supplier	A supply chain is the system of organizations, people, technology, activities, information and resources involved in moving a product or service from Supplier to customer. Supply chain activities transform natural resources, raw materials and components into a finished product that is delivered to the end customer. In sophisticated supply chain systems, used products may re-enter the supply chain at any point where residual value is recyclable.
Original equipment manufacturer	An Original equipment manufacturer, manufactures products or components which are purchased by a second company and retailed under the second company"s brand name. It is a form of outsourcing. When referring to automotive parts, Original equipment manufacturer designates a replacement part made by the manufacturer of the original part.
BlackBerry	BlackBerry is a line of wireless handheld devices that was introduced in 1999 as a two-way pager. In 2002, the more commonly known smartphone BlackBerry was released, which supports push e-mail, mobile telephone, text messaging, internet faxing, web browsing and other wireless information services. It is an example of a convergent device.
Inventory	Inventory is a list for goods and materials, held available in stock by a business. It is also used for a list of the contents of a household and for a list for testamentary purposes of the possessions of someone who has died. In accounting Inventory is considered an asset.
Raw material	A raw material is something that is acted upon or used by or by human labour or industry, for use as a building material to create some product or structure. Often the term is used to denote material that came from nature and is in an unprocessed or minimally processed state. Iron ore, logs, and crude oil, would be examples.
Procter ' Gamble	Procter is a surname, and may also refer to: · Bryan Waller Procter (pseud. Barry Cornwall), English poet · Goodwin Procter, American law firm · Procter ' Gamble, consumer products multinational "
Celebrity branding	Celebrity branding is a type of branding, in which a celebrity uses his or her status in society to promote a product, service or charity. Celebrity branding can take several different forms, from a celebrity simply appearing in advertisements for a product, service or charity, to a celebrity attending PR events, creating his or her own line of products or services, and/or using his or her name as a brand. The most popular forms of celebrity brand lines are for clothing and fragrances.
Need for Achievement	Need for Achievement (N-Ach) refers to an individual"s desire for significant accomplishment, mastering of skills, control, David McClelland. Need for Achievement is related to the difficulty of tasks people choose to undertake.

Dangerous goods	Dangerous goods,), are solids, liquids, other living organisms, property, or the environment. They are often subject to chemical regulations. dangerous goods include materials that are radioactive, flammable, explosive or corrosive, oxidizers or asphyxiants, biohazardous, toxic, pathogen or allergen substances and organisms.
Product	When a product reaches the maturity stage of the product life cycle a company may choose to operate strategies to extend the life of the product. If the product is predicted to continue to be successful or an upgrade is soon to be released the company can use various methods to keep sales, else the product will be left as is to continue to the decline stage.
	Examples of extension strategies are:
	· Discounted price
	· Increased advertising
	· Accessing another market abroad
	Another strategy is added value.
	This is a widely used extension strategy.

Purchasing	Purchasing refers to a business or organization attempting to acquire goods or services to accomplish the goals of the enterprise. Though there are several organizations that attempt to set standards in the Purchasing process, processes can vary greatly between organizations. Typically the word "Purchasing" is not used interchangeably with the word "procurement", since procurement typically includes Expediting, Supplier Quality, and Traffic and Logistics (T'L) in addition to Purchasing.
Distribution	Distribution (or place) is one of the four elements of marketing mix. An organization or set of organizations (go-betweens) involved in the process of making a product or service available for use or consumption by a consumer or business user. The other three parts of the marketing mix are product, pricing, and promotion.
Free Trade	Free trade is a type of trade policy that allows traders to act and transact without interference from government. According to the law of comparative advantage the policy permits trading partners mutual gains from trade of goods and services. Under a Free trade policy, prices are a reflection of true supply and demand, and are the sole determinant of resource allocation.
Free Trade Agreement	A Free trade agreement is a trade treaty between two or more countries. Usually these agreements are between two countries and are meant to reduce or completely remove tariffs to trade. According to the World Trade Organization there are more than 200 Free trade agreements in force.
NAFTA	The NAFTA is an agreement signed by the governments of the United States, Canada, and Mexico creating a trilateral trade bloc in North America. The agreement came into force on January 1, 1994. It superseded the Canada-United States Free Trade Agreement between the U.S. and Canada. In terms of combined purchasing power parity GDP of its members, as of 2007 the trade block is the largest in the world and second largest by nominal GDP comparison. The NAFTA (NAFTA) has two supplements, the North American Agreement on Environmental Cooperation (NAAEC) and the North American Agreement on Labor Cooperation (NAALC).
NAICS	The NAICS is used by business and government to classify and measure economic activity in Canada, Mexico and the United States. It has largely replaced the older Standard Industrial Classification system; however, certain government departments and agencies, such as the U.S. Securities and Exchange Commission (SEC), still use the SIC codes. The NAICS numbering system is a six-digit code.
North American Free Trade Agreement	The North American Free Trade Agreement is an agreement signed by the governments of the United States, Canada, and Mexico creating a trilateral trade bloc in North America. The agreement came into force on January 1, 1994. It superseded the Canada-United States Free Trade Agreement between the U.S. and Canada. In terms of combined purchasing power parity GDP of its members, as of 2007 the trade block is the largest in the world and second largest by nominal GDP comparison. The North American Free Trade Agreement has two supplements, the North American Agreement on Environmental Cooperation (NAAEC) and the North American Agreement on Labor Cooperation (NAALC).

Supply chain	A Supply chain or logistics network is the system of organizations, people, technology, activities, information and resources involved in moving a product or service from supplier to customer. Supply chain activities transform natural resources, raw materials and components into a finished product that is delivered to the end customer. In sophisticated Supply chain systems, used products may re-enter the Supply chain at any point where residual value is recyclable.
Procurement	Procurement is the acquisition of goods and/or services at the best possible total cost of ownership, in the right quality and quantity, at the right time, in the right place and from the right source for the direct benefit or use of corporations, individuals, generally via a contract, or it can be the same way selection for human resource Simple Procurement may involve nothing more than repeat purchasing. Complex Procurement could involve finding long term partners - or even "co-destiny" suppliers that might fundamentally commit one organization to another. Almost all purchasing decisions include factors such as delivery and handling, marginal benefit, and price fluctuations.
Goal	A Goal or objective is a projected state of affairs that a person or a system plans or intends to achieve--a personal or organizational desired end-point in some sort of assumed development. Many people endeavor to reach Goals within a finite time by setting deadlines. A desire or an intention becomes a Goal if and only if one activates an action for achieving it .
Dangerous goods	Dangerous goods,), are solids, liquids, other living organisms, property, or the environment. They are often subject to chemical regulations. dangerous goods include materials that are radioactive, flammable, explosive or corrosive, oxidizers or asphyxiants, biohazardous, toxic, pathogen or allergen substances and organisms.
Total cost	In economics, and cost accounting, Total cost describes the total economic cost of production and is made up of variable costs, which vary according to the quantity of a good produced and include inputs such as labor and raw materials, plus fixed costs, which are independent of the quantity of a good produced and include inputs (capital) that cannot be varied in the short term, such as buildings and machinery. Total cost in economics includes the total opportunity cost of each factor of production in addition to fixed and variable costs. The rate at which Total cost changes as the amount produced changes is called marginal cost.
Value	A personal and cultural value is a relative ethic value, an assumption upon which implementation can be extrapolated. A value system is a set of consistent values and measures that is soo not true. A principle value is a foundation upon which other values and measures of integrity are based.
Complexity	One of the problems in addressing Complexity issues has been distinguishing conceptually between the large number of variances in relationships extant in random collections, and the , but smaller, number of relationships between elements in systems where constraints (related to correlation of otherwise independent elements) simultaneously reduce the variations from element independence and create distinguishable regimes of more-uniform, relationships, or interactions. Weaver perceived and addressed this problem, in at least a preliminary way, in drawing a distinction between "disorganized Complexity" and "organized Complexity".

In Weaver"s view, disorganized Complexity results from the particular system having a very large number of parts, say millions of parts, or many more.

Total cost of ownership	Total cost of ownership is a financial estimate designed to help consumers and enterprise managers assess direct and indirect costs It is a form of full cost accounting.
Value engineering	Value engineering is a systematic method to improve the "value" of goods or products and services by using an examination of function. Value, as defined, is the ratio of function to cost. Value can therefore be increased by either improving the function or reducing the cost.
Supplier	A supply chain is the system of organizations, people, technology, activities, information and resources involved in moving a product or service from Supplier to customer. Supply chain activities transform natural resources, raw materials and components into a finished product that is delivered to the end customer. In sophisticated supply chain systems, used products may re-enter the supply chain at any point where residual value is recyclable.
Collaboration	Collaboration is a recursive process where two or more people or organizations work together in an intersection of common goals -- for example, an intellectual endeavor that is creative in nature--by sharing knowledge, learning and building consensus. Most Collaboration requires leadership, although the form of leadership can be social within a decentralized and egalitarian group. In particular, teams that work collaboratively can obtain greater resources, recognition and reward when facing competition for finite resources.Collaboration is also present in opposing goals exhibiting the notion of adversarial Collaboration, though this is not a common case for using the term.
Determinant	In algebra, the determinant is a special number associated to any square matrix, that is to say, a rectangular array of numbers where the (finite) number of rows and columns are equal. The fundamental geometric meaning of a determinant is a scale factor for measure when the matrix is regarded as a linear transformation. Thus a 2×2 matrix with determinant 2 when applied to a set of points with finite area will transform those points into a set with twice the area.
Forecasting	Forecasting is the process of estimation in unknown situations. Prediction is a similar, but more general term. Both can refer to estimation of time series, cross-sectional or longitudinal data.
New product development	In business and engineering, new product development is the term used to describe the complete process of bringing a new product or service to market. There are two parallel paths involved in the new product development process: one involves the idea generation, product design, and detail engineering; the other involves market research and marketing analysis. Companies typically see new product development as the first stage in generating and commercializing new products within the overall strategic process of product life cycle management used to maintain or grow their market share. · Idea Generation is often called the "fuzzy front end" of the new product development process

· Ideas for new products can be obtained from basic research using a SWOT analysis (Strengths, Weaknesses, Opportunities ' Threats), Market and consumer trends, company"s R'D department, competitors, focus groups, employees, salespeople, corporate spies, trade shows, or Ethnographic discovery methods (searching for user patterns and habits) may also be used to get an insight into new product lines or product features.

· Idea Generation or Brainstorming of new product, service, or store concepts - idea generation techniques can begin when you have done your OPPORTUNITY ANALYSIS to support your ideas in the Idea Screening Phase (shown in the next development step).

· Idea Screening

· The object is to eliminate unsound concepts prior to devoting resources to them.
· The screeners must ask at least three questions:

· Will the customer in the target market benefit from the product?
· What is the size and growth forecasts of the market segment/target market?
· What is the current or expected competitive pressure for the product idea?
· What are the industry sales and market trends the product idea is based on?
· Is it technically feasible to manufacture the product?
· Will the product be profitable when manufactured and delivered to the customer at the target price?
· Concept Development and Testing

· Develop the marketing and engineering details

· Who is the target market and who is the decision maker in the purchasing process?
· What product features must the product incorporate?
· What benefits will the product provide?
· How will consumers react to the product?
· How will the product be produced most cost effectively?
· Prove feasibility through virtual computer aided rendering, and rapid prototyping
· What will it cost to produce it?
· Testing the Concept by asking a sample of prospective customers what they think of the idea.

| Product | When a product reaches the maturity stage of the product life cycle a company may choose to operate strategies to extend the life of the product. If the product is predicted to continue to be successful or an upgrade is soon to be released the company can use various methods to keep sales, else the product will be left as is to continue to the decline stage. |

Examples of extension strategies are:

· Discounted price
· Increased advertising
· Accessing another market abroad
Another strategy is added value.
This is a widely used extension strategy.

Sale	A sale is the pinnacle activity involved in selling products or services in return for money or other compensation. It is an act of completion of a commercial activity. A sale is completed by the seller, the owner of the goods.
Value-based pricing	Value-based pricing, or Value optimized pricing is a business strategy. It sets selling prices on the perceived value to the customer, rather than on the actual cost of the product, the market price, competitors prices, or the historical price. The goal of Value-based pricing is to align price with value delivered.
Need for Achievement	Need for Achievement (N-Ach) refers to an individual"s desire for significant accomplishment, mastering of skills, control, David McClelland. Need for Achievement is related to the difficulty of tasks people choose to undertake.
Marketing	marketing is a "social and managerial process by which individuals and groups obtain what they need and want through creating and exchanging products and values with others." It is an integrated process through which companies create value for customers and build strong customer relationships in order to capture value from customers in return. marketing is used to create the customer, to keep the customer and to satisfy the customer. With the customer as the focus of its activities, it can be concluded that marketing management is one of the major components of business management.
Accounting profit	Accounting profit is the difference between price and the costs of bringing to market whatever it is that is accounted as an enterprise (whether by harvest, extraction, manufacture) in terms of the component costs of delivered goods and/or services and any operating or other expenses. A key difficulty in measuring profit is in defining costs. Pure economic monetary profits can be zero or negative even in competitive equilibrium when accounted monetized costs exceed monetized price.
E-procurement	E-procurement (electronic procurement,) is the business-to-business or business-to-consumer or Business-to-government purchase and sale of supplies, Work and services through the Internet as well as other information and networking systems, such as Electronic Data Interchange and Enterprise Resource Planning. Typically, e-procurement Web sites allow qualified and registered users to look for buyers or sellers of goods and services. Depending on the approach, buyers or sellers may specify costs or invite bids.
Best practice	A best practice is a technique, method, process, activity, incentive or reward that is believed to be more effective at delivering a particular outcome than any other technique, method, process, etc. The idea is that with proper processes, checks, and testing, a desired outcome can be delivered with fewer problems and unforeseen complications. best practices can also be defined as the most efficient (least amount of effort) and effective (best results) way of accomplishing a task, based on repeatable procedures that have proven themselves over time for large numbers of people.

Relationship management	Customer Relationship management (C Relationship management) consists of the processes a company uses to track and organize its contacts with its current and prospective customers. C Relationship management software is used to support these processes; information about customers and customer interactions can be entered, stored and accessed by employees in different company departments. Typical C Relationship management goals are to improve services provided to customers, and to use customer contact information for targeted marketing.
Defined	In mathematics, Defined and unDefined are used to explain whether or not expressions have meaningful, sensible, and unambiguous values. Whether an expression has a meaningful value depends on the context of the expression. For example the value of 4 − 5 is unDefined if a positive integer result is required.
Measure theory	In mathematics, more specifically in measure theory, a measure on a set is a systematic way to assign to each suitable subset a number, intuitively interpreted as the size of the subset. In this sense, a measure is a generalization of the concepts of length, area and volume. A particularly important example is the Lebesgue measure on a Euclidean space, which assigns the conventional length, area and volume of Euclidean geometry to suitable subsets of R^n, n=1,2,3,....
Reverse auction	A Reverse auction is a tool used in industrial business-to-business procurement. It is a type of auction in which the role of the buyer and seller are reversed, with the primary objective to drive purchase prices downward. In an ordinary auction, buyers compete to obtain a good or service.
Business marketing	Business marketing is the practice of individuals, or organizations, including commercial businesses, governments and institutions, facilitating the sale of their products or services to other companies or organizations that in turn resell them, use them as components in products or services they offer or use them to support their operations. Also known as industrial marketing, Business marketing is also called business-to-Business marketing, or B2B marketing, for short. (Note that while marketing to government entities shares some of the same dynamics of organizational marketing, B2G Marketing is meaningfully different).
Marketing Ethics	Marketing ethics is the area of applied ethics which deals with the moral principles behind the operation and regulation of marketing. Some areas of Marketing ethics (ethics of advertising and promotion) overlap with media ethics. Possible frameworks: · Value-oriented framework, analyzing ethical problems on the basis of the values which they infringe (e.g. honesty, autonomy, privacy, transparency). An example of such an approach is the AMA Statement of Ethics. · Stakeholder-oriented framework, analysing ethical problems on the basis of whom they affect (e.g. consumers, competitors, society as a whole). · Process-oriented framework, analysing ethical problems in terms of the categories used by marketing specialists (e.g. research, price, promotion, placement).

Contract	In common-law systems, the five key requirements for the creation of a Contract are: 1. offer and acceptance (agreement) 2. consideration 3. an intention to create legal relations 4. legal capacity 5. formalities
	In civil-law systems, the concept of consideration is not central. In addition, for some Contracts formalities must be complied with under what is sometimes called a statute of frauds.
	One of the most famous cases on forming a Contract is Carlill v. Carbolic Smoke Ball Company, decided in nineteenth-century England.
Publication	The word publication means the act of publishing, and it also means any writing of which copies are published, and any website. Among publication s are books, and periodicals, the latter including magazines, scholarly journals, and newspapers.
	publication is a technical term in legal contexts and especially important in copyright legislation.
Celebrity branding	Celebrity branding is a type of branding, in which a celebrity uses his or her status in society to promote a product, service or charity. Celebrity branding can take several different forms, from a celebrity simply appearing in advertisements for a product, service or charity, to a celebrity attending PR events, creating his or her own line of products or services, and/or using his or her name as a brand. The most popular forms of celebrity brand lines are for clothing and fragrances.
Strategy	A Strategy is a plan of action designed to achieve a particular goal.
	Strategy is different from tactics. In military terms, tactics is concerned with the conduct of an engagement while Strategy is concerned with how different engagements are linked.
Targeted advertising	Targeted advertising is a type of advertising whereby advertisements are placed so as to reach consumers based on various traits such as demographics, purchase history, or observed behavior.
	Two principal forms of targeted interactive advertising are behavioral targeting and contextual advertising.

Strategy	A Strategy is a plan of action designed to achieve a particular goal.
	Strategy is different from tactics. In military terms, tactics is concerned with the conduct of an engagement while Strategy is concerned with how different engagements are linked.
Supplier	A supply chain is the system of organizations, people, technology, activities, information and resources involved in moving a product or service from Supplier to customer. Supply chain activities transform natural resources, raw materials and components into a finished product that is delivered to the end customer. In sophisticated supply chain systems, used products may re-enter the supply chain at any point where residual value is recyclable.
Marketing	marketing is a "social and managerial process by which individuals and groups obtain what they need and want through creating and exchanging products and values with others." It is an integrated process through which companies create value for customers and build strong customer relationships in order to capture value from customers in return.
	marketing is used to create the customer, to keep the customer and to satisfy the customer. With the customer as the focus of its activities, it can be concluded that marketing management is one of the major components of business management.
Relationship management	Customer Relationship management (C Relationship management) consists of the processes a company uses to track and organize its contacts with its current and prospective customers. C Relationship management software is used to support these processes; information about customers and customer interactions can be entered, stored and accessed by employees in different company departments. Typical C Relationship management goals are to improve services provided to customers, and to use customer contact information for targeted marketing.
Selection	In the context of evolution, certain traits or alleles of a species may be subject to selection. Under selection, individuals with advantageous or "adaptive" traits tend to be more successful than their peers reproductively--meaning they contribute more offspring to the succeeding generation than others do. When these traits have a genetic basis, selection can increase the prevalence of those traits, because offspring will inherit those traits from their parents.
Mind control	Mind control (also referred to as brainwashing, coercive persuasion, and thought reform) refers to a broad range of psychological tactics thought to subvert an individual"s control of his or her own thinking, behavior, emotions).
Purchasing	Purchasing refers to a business or organization attempting to acquire goods or services to accomplish the goals of the enterprise. Though there are several organizations that attempt to set standards in the Purchasing process, processes can vary greatly between organizations. Typically the word "Purchasing" is not used interchangeably with the word "procurement", since procurement typically includes Expediting, Supplier Quality, and Traffic and Logistics (T'L) in addition to Purchasing.

Resources	Human beings are also considered to be Resources because they have the ability to change raw materials into valuable Resources. The term Human Resources can also be defined as the skills, energies, talents, abilities and knowledge that are used for the production of goods or the rendering of services. While taking into account human beings as Resources, the following things have to be kept in mind: · The size of the population · The capabilities of the individuals in that population Many Resources cannot be consumed in their original form. They have to be processed in order to change them into more usable commodities.
Technology	Technology is a broad concept that deals with an animal species" usage and knowledge of tools and crafts, and how it affects an animal species" ability to control and adapt to its environment. Technology is a term with origins in the Greek "technologia", "τεχνολογÎÂ¯α" -- "techne", "τîÂχνη" and "logia", "λογÎÂ¯α" ("saying".) However, a strict definition is elusive; "Technology" can refer to material objects of use to humanity, such as machines, hardware or utensils, but can also encompass broader themes, including systems, methods of organization, and techniques.
Procurement	Procurement is the acquisition of goods and/or services at the best possible total cost of ownership, in the right quality and quantity, at the right time, in the right place and from the right source for the direct benefit or use of corporations, individuals, generally via a contract, or it can be the same way selection for human resource Simple Procurement may involve nothing more than repeat purchasing. Complex Procurement could involve finding long term partners - or even "co-destiny" suppliers that might fundamentally commit one organization to another. Almost all purchasing decisions include factors such as delivery and handling, marginal benefit, and price fluctuations.
Activism	Activism, in a general sense, can be described as intentional action to bring about social change, political change, economic justice, or opposition to, one side of an often controversial argument. The word "Activism" is often used synonymously with protest or dissent, but Activism can stem from any number of political orientations and take a wide range of forms, from writing letters to newspapers or politicians, political campaigning, economic Activism (such as boycotts or preferentially patronizing preferred businesses), rallies, street marches, strikes, both work stoppages and hunger strikes, or even guerrilla tactics.
Internet marketing	Internet marketing, also referred to as i-marketing, web marketing, online marketing, is the marketing of products, or, services over the Internet. The Internet has brought media to a global audience. The interactive nature of Internet marketing, both, in terms of providing instant response and eliciting responses, is a unique quality of the medium.

Best practice	A best practice is a technique, method, process, activity, incentive or reward that is believed to be more effective at delivering a particular outcome than any other technique, method, process, etc. The idea is that with proper processes, checks, and testing, a desired outcome can be delivered with fewer problems and unforeseen complications. best practices can also be defined as the most efficient (least amount of effort) and effective (best results) way of accomplishing a task, based on repeatable procedures that have proven themselves over time for large numbers of people.
Product	When a product reaches the maturity stage of the product life cycle a company may choose to operate strategies to extend the life of the product. If the product is predicted to continue to be successful or an upgrade is soon to be released the company can use various methods to keep sales, else the product will be left as is to continue to the decline stage. Examples of extension strategies are: · Discounted price · Increased advertising · Accessing another market abroad Another strategy is added value. This is a widely used extension strategy.
Product development	In business and engineering, new Product development (NPD) is the term used to describe the complete process of bringing a new product or service to market. There are two parallel paths involved in the NPD process: one involves the idea generation, product design, and detail engineering; the other involves market research and marketing analysis. Companies typically see new Product development as the first stage in generating and commercializing new products within the overall strategic process of product life cycle management used to maintain or grow their market share. · Idea Generation is often called the "fuzzy front end" of the NPD process · Ideas for new products can be obtained from basic research using a SWOT analysis (Strengths, Weaknesses, Opportunities ' Threats), Market and consumer trends, company"s R'D department, competitors, focus groups, employees, salespeople, corporate spies, trade shows, or Ethnographic discovery methods (searching for user patterns and habits) may also be used to get an insight into new product lines or product features. · Idea Generation or Brainstorming of new product, service, or store concepts - idea generation techniques can begin when you have done your OPPORTUNITY ANALYSIS to support your ideas in the Idea Screening Phase (shown in the next development step). · Idea Screening · The object is to eliminate unsound concepts prior to devoting resources to them. · The screeners must ask at least three questions:

· Will the customer in the target market benefit from the product?

· What is the size and growth forecasts of the market segment/target market?

· What is the current or expected competitive pressure for the product idea?

· What are the industry sales and market trends the product idea is based on?

· Is it technically feasible to manufacture the product?

· Will the product be profitable when manufactured and delivered to the customer at the target price?

· Concept Development and Testing

· Develop the marketing and engineering details

· Who is the target market and who is the decision maker in the purchasing process?

· What product features must the product incorporate?

· What benefits will the product provide?

· How will consumers react to the product?

· How will the product be produced most cost effectively?

· Prove feasibility through virtual computer aided rendering, and rapid prototyping

· What will it cost to produce it?

· Testing the Concept by asking a sample of prospective customers what they think of the idea.

Solution	In chemistry, a solution is a homogeneous mixture composed of two or more substances. In such a mixture, a solute is dissolved in another substance, known as a solvent. Gases may dissolve in liquids, for example, carbon dioxide or oxygen in water.
Walt Disney	Walter Elias "Walt" Disney (December 5, 1901 - December 15, 1966) was an American film producer, director, screenwriter, voice actor, animator, entrepreneur, entertainer, international icon and philanthropist. Disney is famous for his influence in the field of entertainment during the twentieth century. As the co-founder (with his brother Roy O. Disney) of Walt Disney Productions, Disney became one of the best-known motion picture producers in the world.
Walt Disney Company	The Walt Disney Company is the largest media and entertainment corporation in the world. Founded on October 16, 1923, by brothers Walt and Roy Disney as an animation studio, it has become one of the biggest Hollywood studios, and owner and licensor of eleven theme parks and several television networks, including ABC and ESPN. Disney"s corporate headquarters and primary production facilities are located at The Walt Disney Studios in Burbank, California.
Role	A role or a social role is a set of connected behaviors, rights and obligations as conceptualized by actors in a social situation. It is an expected behavior in a given individual social status and social position. It is vital to both functionalist and interactionist understandings of society.
Pseudo-evaluation	Pseudo-evaluation

Politically controlled and public relations studies are based on an objectivist epistemology from an elite perspective. Although both of these approaches seek to misrepresent value interpretations about some object, they go about it a bit differently. Information obtained through politically controlled studies is released or withheld to meet the special interests of the holder.

| Functional selectivity | Functional selectivity (or "agonist trafficking", "biased agonism", "differential engagement" and "protean agonism") is the ligand-dependent selectivity for certain signal transduction pathways in one and the same receptor. This can be present when a receptor has several possible signal transduction pathways. To which degree each pathway is activated thus depends on which ligand binds to the receptor . |

| Self-sufficiency | Self-sufficiency refers to the state of not requiring any outside aid, support for survival; it is therefore a type of personal or collective autonomy. On a large scale, a totally self-sufficient economy that does not trade with the outside world is called an autarky.

 The term Self-sufficiency is usually applied to varieties of sustainable living in which nothing is consumed outside of what is produced by the self-sufficient individuals. |

Relationship marketing	Relationship marketing is a form of marketing developed from direct response marketing campaigns conducted in the 1970"s and 1980"s which emphasizes customer retention and satisfaction, rather than a dominant focus on "point of sale" transactions. relationship marketing differs from other forms of marketing in that it recognizes the long term value to the firm of keeping customers, as opposed to direct or "Intrusion" marketing, which focuses upon acquisition of new clients by targeting majority demographics based upon prospective client lists. relationship marketing refers to long-term and mutually beneficial arrangement wherein both buyer and seller focus on value enhancement through the certain of more satisfying exchange.This approach attempts to transcend the simple purchase exchange process with customer to make more meaningful and richer contact by providing a more holistic, personalized purchase, and use orn consumption experience to create stronger ties.
Operational	An operational definition is a demonstration of a process - such as a variable, term). Properties described in this manner must be sufficiently accessible, so that persons other than the definer may independently measure or test for them at will.
Transactional	A transaction is an agreement, communication, often involving the exchange of items of value, such as information, goods, services, and money. · Financial transaction · Real estate transaction · Transaction cost · Database transaction · Atomic database transaction · Transaction processing · POS Transaction Transaction may also refer to: · Transaction Publishers · "Transaction," an episode of the Death Note anime series, see List of Death Note episodes · transactional analysis, a psychoanalytic theory of psychology · transactional interpretation, an interpretation of quantum mechanics. "
Linkage	Linkage generally means "the manner or style of being united", and can refer to: · Genetic Linkage · Linkage (mechanical) · Linkage (policy) · Linkage (linguistics) · Linkage (software) · Linkage (BitTorrent client) · Linkage is also a commonly used phrase in most instant message programs used to request a URL or hyperlink to a web location, particularly a hyperlink to a photo of a person, particularly on a social website such as facebook or myspace. It is used on some websites in place of a "link to us" (or similar) text.

	· Also see webpage and web browser "
Stereotype	A stereotype is a commonly held public belief about specific social groups, based on some prior assumptions.
Best practice	A best practice is a technique, method, process, activity, incentive or reward that is believed to be more effective at delivering a particular outcome than any other technique, method, process, etc. The idea is that with proper processes, checks, and testing, a desired outcome can be delivered with fewer problems and unforeseen complications. best practices can also be defined as the most efficient (least amount of effort) and effective (best results) way of accomplishing a task, based on repeatable procedures that have proven themselves over time for large numbers of people.
Relationship management	Customer Relationship management (C Relationship management) consists of the processes a company uses to track and organize its contacts with its current and prospective customers. C Relationship management software is used to support these processes; information about customers and customer interactions can be entered, stored and accessed by employees in different company departments. Typical C Relationship management goals are to improve services provided to customers, and to use customer contact information for targeted marketing.
Supplier	A supply chain is the system of organizations, people, technology, activities, information and resources involved in moving a product or service from Supplier to customer. Supply chain activities transform natural resources, raw materials and components into a finished product that is delivered to the end customer. In sophisticated supply chain systems, used products may re-enter the supply chain at any point where residual value is recyclable.
Switching cost	Switching barriers or Switching cost s are terms used in microeconomics, strategic management, and marketing to describe any impediment to a customer"s changing of suppliers. In many markets, consumers are forced to incur costs when switching from one supplier to another. These costs are called Switching cost s and can come in many different shapes.
Value	A personal and cultural value is a relative ethic value, an assumption upon which implementation can be extrapolated. A value system is a set of consistent values and measures that is soo not true. A principle value is a foundation upon which other values and measures of integrity are based.
Strategy	A Strategy is a plan of action designed to achieve a particular goal. Strategy is different from tactics. In military terms, tactics is concerned with the conduct of an engagement while Strategy is concerned with how different engagements are linked.
Activity-based costing	Activity-based costing (ABC) is a costing model that identifies activities in an organization and assigns the cost of each activity resource to all products and services according to the actual consumption by each: it assigns more indirect costs (overhead) into direct costs.

In this way an organization can precisely estimate the cost of its individual products and services for the purposes of identifying and eliminating those which are unprofitable and lowering the prices of those which are overpriced.

In a business organization, the ABC methodology assigns an organization"s resource costs through activities to the products and services provided to its customers.

Customer profitability

Customer profitability is the difference between the revenues earned from and the costs associated with the customer relationship in a specified period.

According to Philip Kotler,"a profitable customer is a person, household or a company that overtime, yields a revenue stream that exceeds by an acceptable amount the company"s cost stream of attracting, selling and servicing the customer"

Although Customer profitability is nothing more than the result of applying the business concept of profit to a customer relationship, measuring the profitability of a firm"s customers or customer groups can often deliver useful business insights.

Quite often a very small percentage of the firm"s best customers will account for a large portion of firm profit.

Net margin

Profit margin, net margin, net profit margin or net profit ratio all refer to a measure of profitability. It is calculated by finding the net profit as a percentage of the revenue.

$$\text{Net profit margin} = \frac{\text{Net profit (after taxes)}}{\text{Revenue}} \times 100\%$$

The profit margin is mostly used for internal comparison.

Dangerous goods

Dangerous goods,), are solids, liquids, other living organisms, property, or the environment. They are often subject to chemical regulations. dangerous goods include materials that are radioactive, flammable, explosive or corrosive, oxidizers or asphyxiants, biohazardous, toxic, pathogen or allergen substances and organisms.

Defined

In mathematics, Defined and unDefined are used to explain whether or not expressions have meaningful, sensible, and unambiguous values. Whether an expression has a meaningful value depends on the context of the expression. For example the value of 4 − 5 is unDefined if a positive integer result is required.

Sale

A sale is the pinnacle activity involved in selling products or services in return for money or other compensation. It is an act of completion of a commercial activity.

A sale is completed by the seller, the owner of the goods.

Technology

Technology is a broad concept that deals with an animal species" usage and knowledge of tools and crafts, and how it affects an animal species" ability to control and adapt to its environment. Technology is a term with origins in the Greek "technologia", "τεχνολογÎ⁻α" -- "techne", "τÎχνη" and "logia", "λογÎ⁻α" ("saying".) However, a strict definition is elusive; "Technology" can refer to material objects of use to humanity, such as machines, hardware or utensils, but can also encompass broader themes, including systems, methods of organization, and techniques.

Consumer	Consumer is a broad label for any individuals or households that use goods and services generated within the economy. The concept of a Consumer is used in different contexts, so that the usage and significance of the term may vary.
	Typically when business people and economists talk of Consumers they are talking about person as Consumer, an aggregated commodity item with little individuality other than that expressed in the buy/not-buy decision.
Need for Achievement	Need for Achievement (N-Ach) refers to an individual"s desire for significant accomplishment, mastering of skills, control, David McClelland.
	Need for Achievement is related to the difficulty of tasks people choose to undertake.
Value proposition	In the field of marketing, a customer Value proposition consists of the sum total of benefits which a vendor promises that a customer will receive in return for the customer"s associated payment (or other value-transfer.)
	Put simply, the Value proposition is what the customer gets for his money.
	Accordingly, a customer can evaluate a company"s value-proposition on two broad dimensions with multiple subsets:
	· relative performance: what the customer gets from the vendor relative to a competitor"s offering; · price: which consists of the payment the customer makes to acquire the product or service; plus the access cost
	The vendor-company"s marketing and sales efforts offer a customer Value proposition; the vendor-company"s delivery and customer-service processes then fulfill that value-proposition.
	A value-proposition can assist in a firm"s marketing strategy, and may guide a business to target a particular market segment.
Employee	Employment is a contract between two parties, one being the employer and the other being the employee. An employee may be defined as: "A person in the service of another under any contract of hire, express or implied, oral or written, where the employer has the power or right to control and direct the employee in the material details of how the work is to be performed." Black"s Law Dictionary page 471 (5th ed. 1979).
	In a commercial setting, the employer conceives of a productive activity, generally with the intention of generating a profit, and the employee contributes labour to the enterprise, usually in return for payment of wages.
Strategic alliance	A strategic alliance is a formal relationship between two or more parties to pursue a set of agreed upon goals or to meet a critical business need while remaining independent organizations.

Partners may provide the strategic alliance with resources such as products, distribution channels, manufacturing capability, project funding, capital equipment, knowledge, expertise, or intellectual property. The alliance is a cooperation or collaboration which aims for a synergy where each partner hopes that the benefits from the alliance will be greater than those from individual efforts.

Determinant	In algebra, the determinant is a special number associated to any square matrix, that is to say, a rectangular array of numbers where the (finite) number of rows and columns are equal. The fundamental geometric meaning of a determinant is a scale factor for measure when the matrix is regarded as a linear transformation. Thus a 2 × 2 matrix with determinant 2 when applied to a set of points with finite area will transform those points into a set with twice the area.
Contract	In common-law systems, the five key requirements for the creation of a Contract are: 1. offer and acceptance (agreement) 2. consideration 3. an intention to create legal relations 4. legal capacity 5. formalities In civil-law systems, the concept of consideration is not central. In addition, for some Contracts formalities must be complied with under what is sometimes called a statute of frauds. One of the most famous cases on forming a Contract is Carlill v. Carbolic Smoke Ball Company, decided in nineteenth-century England.
Goal	A Goal or objective is a projected state of affairs that a person or a system plans or intends to achieve--a personal or organizational desired end-point in some sort of assumed development. Many people endeavor to reach Goals within a finite time by setting deadlines. A desire or an intention becomes a Goal if and only if one activates an action for achieving it .
Supply chain	A Supply chain or logistics network is the system of organizations, people, technology, activities, information and resources involved in moving a product or service from supplier to customer. Supply chain activities transform natural resources, raw materials and components into a finished product that is delivered to the end customer. In sophisticated Supply chain systems, used products may re-enter the Supply chain at any point where residual value is recyclable.
Sony	Sony Corporation is a multinational conglomerate corporation headquartered in Minato, Tokyo, Japan, and one of the world"s largest media conglomerates with revenue exceeding US$99.1 billion . Sony is one of the leading manufacturers of electronics, video, communications, video game consoles, and information technology products for the consumer and professional markets. Sony Corporation is the electronics business unit and the parent company of the Sony Group, which is engaged in business through its five operating segments--electronics, games, entertainment (motion pictures and music), financial services and other.
Solution	In chemistry, a solution is a homogeneous mixture composed of two or more substances. In such a mixture, a solute is dissolved in another substance, known as a solvent. Gases may dissolve in liquids, for example, carbon dioxide or oxygen in water.

Opportunities	"opportunities (Let"s Make Lots of Money)" is a song by UK synthpop duo Pet Shop Boys, released as a single in 1985 and then in 1986, gaining greater popularity in both the UK and U.S. with its second release.
	Written as a satire of Thatcherism and its embodiment in conspicuous consumption and yuppies in the United Kingdom during the 1980s, the song"s indirect attack on its subject matter has come to exemplify the Pet Shop Boys as ironists in their songwriting.
	The song was written during the Pet Shop Boys" formative years, in 1983. According to Neil Tennant, the main lyrical concept came while in a recording studio in Camden Town when Chris Lowe asked him to make up a lyric based around the line "Let"s make lots of money".
NAICS	The NAICS is used by business and government to classify and measure economic activity in Canada, Mexico and the United States. It has largely replaced the older Standard Industrial Classification system; however, certain government departments and agencies, such as the U.S. Securities and Exchange Commission (SEC), still use the SIC codes.
	The NAICS numbering system is a six-digit code.
Value	A personal and cultural value is a relative ethic value, an assumption upon which implementation can be extrapolated. A value system is a set of consistent values and measures that is soo not true. A principle value is a foundation upon which other values and measures of integrity are based.
Purchasing	Purchasing refers to a business or organization attempting to acquire goods or services to accomplish the goals of the enterprise. Though there are several organizations that attempt to set standards in the Purchasing process, processes can vary greatly between organizations. Typically the word "Purchasing" is not used interchangeably with the word "procurement", since procurement typically includes Expediting, Supplier Quality, and Traffic and Logistics (T'L) in addition to Purchasing.
Value-based pricing	Value-based pricing, or Value optimized pricing is a business strategy. It sets selling prices on the perceived value to the customer, rather than on the actual cost of the product, the market price, competitors prices, or the historical price.
	The goal of Value-based pricing is to align price with value delivered.
Business model	A Business model describes the rational of how an organization creates, delivers, and captures value - economic, social, including purpose, offerings, strategies, infrastructure, organizational structures, trading practices, and operational processes and policies.
	Conceptualization of models try to formalize informal descriptions into building blocks and their over business activities. While many different conceptualizations exist, Osterwalder proposed, Thesis by Alexander Osterwalder, 2004 a synthesis of different conceptualizations into a single reference model based on the similarities of a large range of models, and constitutes a Business model design template which allows enterprises to describe their Business model:
	Business model design template: Nine building blocks and their relationships, Osterwalder 2004
	Infrastructure

	· Core capabilities:The capabilities and competencies necessary to execute a company"s Business model. · Partner network: The business alliances which complement other aspects of the Business model.
Toyota	Toyota Motor Corporation is a multinational corporation headquartered in Japan, and currently the world"s largest automaker. Toyota employs approximately 316,000 people around the world. In 1934, while still a department of Toyota Industries, it created its first product Type A engine and in 1936 its first passenger car the Toyota AA.
Supplier	A supply chain is the system of organizations, people, technology, activities, information and resources involved in moving a product or service from Supplier to customer. Supply chain activities transform natural resources, raw materials and components into a finished product that is delivered to the end customer. In sophisticated supply chain systems, used products may re-enter the supply chain at any point where residual value is recyclable.
Celebrity branding	Celebrity branding is a type of branding, in which a celebrity uses his or her status in society to promote a product, service or charity. Celebrity branding can take several different forms, from a celebrity simply appearing in advertisements for a product, service or charity, to a celebrity attending PR events, creating his or her own line of products or services, and/or using his or her name as a brand. The most popular forms of celebrity brand lines are for clothing and fragrances.
Consumer	Consumer is a broad label for any individuals or households that use goods and services generated within the economy. The concept of a Consumer is used in different contexts, so that the usage and significance of the term may vary. Typically when business people and economists talk of Consumers they are talking about person as Consumer, an aggregated commodity item with little individuality other than that expressed in the buy/not-buy decision.
Product	When a product reaches the maturity stage of the product life cycle a company may choose to operate strategies to extend the life of the product. If the product is predicted to continue to be successful or an upgrade is soon to be released the company can use various methods to keep sales, else the product will be left as is to continue to the decline stage. Examples of extension strategies are: · Discounted price · Increased advertising · Accessing another market abroad Another strategy is added value. This is a widely used extension strategy.

Lighting	Lighting or illumination is the deliberate application of light to achieve some aesthetic or practical effect. lighting includes use of both artificial light sources such as lamps and natural illumination of interiors from daylight. Daylighting (through windows, skylights, etc).
Mind control	Mind control (also referred to as brainwashing, coercive persuasion, and thought reform) refers to a broad range of psychological tactics thought to subvert an individual"s control of his or her own thinking, behavior, emotions).
Personal	A personal ad is an item or notice traditionally in the newspaper, similar to a classified ad but personal in nature. In British English it is also commonly known as an advert in a lonely hearts column. With its rise in popularity, the World Wide Web has also become a common medium for personals, commonly referred to as online dating.
Customer service	Customer service is the provision of service to customers before, during and after a purchase. According to Jamier L. Scott. (2002), "Customer service is a series of activities designed to enhance the level of customer satisfaction - that is, the feeling that a product or service has met the customer expectation." Its importance varies by product, industry and customer; defective or broken merchandise can be exchanged/swapped, often only with a receipt and within a specified time frame.
Customer profitability	Customer profitability is the difference between the revenues earned from and the costs associated with the customer relationship in a specified period. According to Philip Kotler,"a profitable customer is a person, household or a company that overtime, yields a revenue stream that exceeds by an acceptable amount the company"s cost stream of attracting, selling and servicing the customer" Although Customer profitability is nothing more than the result of applying the business concept of profit to a customer relationship, measuring the profitability of a firm"s customers or customer groups can often deliver useful business insights. Quite often a very small percentage of the firm"s best customers will account for a large portion of firm profit.
Strategy	A Strategy is a plan of action designed to achieve a particular goal. Strategy is different from tactics. In military terms, tactics is concerned with the conduct of an engagement while Strategy is concerned with how different engagements are linked.
Supply chain	A Supply chain or logistics network is the system of organizations, people, technology, activities, information and resources involved in moving a product or service from supplier to customer. Supply chain activities transform natural resources, raw materials and components into a finished product that is delivered to the end customer. In sophisticated Supply chain systems, used products may re-enter the Supply chain at any point where residual value is recyclable.

Collaboration	Collaboration is a recursive process where two or more people or organizations work together in an intersection of common goals -- for example, an intellectual endeavor that is creative in nature--by sharing knowledge, learning and building consensus. Most Collaboration requires leadership, although the form of leadership can be social within a decentralized and egalitarian group. In particular, teams that work collaboratively can obtain greater resources, recognition and reward when facing competition for finite resources.Collaboration is also present in opposing goals exhibiting the notion of adversarial Collaboration, though this is not a common case for using the term.
Forecasting	Forecasting is the process of estimation in unknown situations. Prediction is a similar, but more general term. Both can refer to estimation of time series, cross-sectional or longitudinal data.
Sale	A sale is the pinnacle activity involved in selling products or services in return for money or other compensation. It is an act of completion of a commercial activity. A sale is completed by the seller, the owner of the goods.
Relationship management	Customer Relationship management (C Relationship management) consists of the processes a company uses to track and organize its contacts with its current and prospective customers. C Relationship management software is used to support these processes; information about customers and customer interactions can be entered, stored and accessed by employees in different company departments. Typical C Relationship management goals are to improve services provided to customers, and to use customer contact information for targeted marketing.
Time	Time is a component of the measuring system used to sequence events, to compare the durations of events and the intervals between them, and to quantify the motions of objects. time has been a major subject of religion, philosophy, and science, but defining time in a non-controversial manner applicable to all fields of study has consistently eluded the greatest scholars. In physics and other sciences, time is considered one of the few fundamental quantities.
Time series	In statistics, signal processing, and many other fields, a time series is a sequence of data points, measured typically at successive times, spaced at (often uniform) time intervals. time series analysis comprises methods that attempt to understand such time series, often either to understand the underlying context of the data points (Where did they come from? What generated them?), or to make forecasts (predictions). time series forecasting is the use of a model to forecast future events based on known past events: to forecast future data points before they are measured.
Quantitative	A quantitative attribute is one that exists in a range of magnitudes, and can therefore be measured. Measurements of any particular quantitative property are expressed as a specific quantity, referred to as a unit, multiplied by a number. Examples of physical quantities are distance, mass, and time.

Small business

A small business is a business that is independently owned and operated, with a small number of employees and relatively low volume of sales. The legal definition of "small" often varies by country and industry, but is generally under 100 employees in the United States and under 50 employees in the European Union. In comparison, the definition of mid-sized business by the number of employees is generally under 500 in the U.S. and 250 for the European Union.

Business marketing	Business marketing is the practice of individuals, or organizations, including commercial businesses, governments and institutions, facilitating the sale of their products or services to other companies or organizations that in turn resell them, use them as components in products or services they offer or use them to support their operations. Also known as industrial marketing, Business marketing is also called business-to-Business marketing, or B2B marketing, for short. (Note that while marketing to government entities shares some of the same dynamics of organizational marketing, B2G Marketing is meaningfully different).
Case study	A case study is one of several ways of doing research whether it is social science related or even socially related. It is an intensive study of a single group, incident, or community. Other ways include experiments, surveys, or analysis of archival information .
Complexity	One of the problems in addressing Complexity issues has been distinguishing conceptually between the large number of variances in relationships extant in random collections, and the , but smaller, number of relationships between elements in systems where constraints (related to correlation of otherwise independent elements) simultaneously reduce the variations from element independence and create distinguishable regimes of more-uniform, relationships, or interactions. Weaver perceived and addressed this problem, in at least a preliminary way, in drawing a distinction between "disorganized Complexity" and "organized Complexity". In Weaver"s view, disorganized Complexity results from the particular system having a very large number of parts, say millions of parts, or many more.
Role	A role or a social role is a set of connected behaviors, rights and obligations as conceptualized by actors in a social situation. It is an expected behavior in a given individual social status and social position. It is vital to both functionalist and interactionist understandings of society.
Strategy	A Strategy is a plan of action designed to achieve a particular goal. Strategy is different from tactics. In military terms, tactics is concerned with the conduct of an engagement while Strategy is concerned with how different engagements are linked.
Strategic business unit	Strategic business unit or Strategic business unit is understood as a business unit within the overall corporate identity which is distinguishable from other business because it serves a defined external market where management can conduct strategic planning in relation to products and markets. When companies become really large, they are best thought of as being composed of a number of businesses (or Strategic business unit s.) In the broader domain of strategic management, the phrase Strategic business unit came into use in the 1960s, largely as a result of General Electric"s many units.
Mind control	Mind control (also referred to as brainwashing, coercive persuasion, and thought reform) refers to a broad range of psychological tactics thought to subvert an individual"s control of his or her own thinking, behavior, emotions).

Outcome	In game theory, an outcome is a set of moves or strategies taken by the players, the final state of the game is known, as are any relevant payoffs. In a game where chance or a random event is involved, the outcome is not known from only the set of strategies, but is only realized when the random event(s) are realized.
Dangerous goods	Dangerous goods,), are solids, liquids, other living organisms, property, or the environment. They are often subject to chemical regulations. dangerous goods include materials that are radioactive, flammable, explosive or corrosive, oxidizers or asphyxiants, biohazardous, toxic, pathogen or allergen substances and organisms.
Decision making	Decision making can be regarded as an outcome of mental processes (cognitive process) leading to the selection of a course of action among several alternatives. Every decision making process produces a final choice. The output can be an action or an opinion of choice.
Business model	A Business model describes the rational of how an organization creates, delivers, and captures value - economic, social, including purpose, offerings, strategies, infrastructure, organizational structures, trading practices, and operational processes and policies. Conceptualization of models try to formalize informal descriptions into building blocks and their over business activities. While many different conceptualizations exist, Osterwalder proposed, Thesis by Alexander Osterwalder, 2004 a synthesis of different conceptualizations into a single reference model based on the similarities of a large range of models, and constitutes a Business model design template which allows enterprises to describe their Business model: Business model design template: Nine building blocks and their relationships, Osterwalder 2004 Infrastructure · Core capabilities:The capabilities and competencies necessary to execute a company"s Business model. · Partner network: The business alliances which complement other aspects of the Business model.
Marketing	marketing is a "social and managerial process by which individuals and groups obtain what they need and want through creating and exchanging products and values with others." It is an integrated process through which companies create value for customers and build strong customer relationships in order to capture value from customers in return. marketing is used to create the customer, to keep the customer and to satisfy the customer. With the customer as the focus of its activities, it can be concluded that marketing management is one of the major components of business management.
Positioning	In marketing, positioning has come to mean the process by which marketers try to create an image or identity in the minds of their target market for its product, brand, or organization. It is the "relative competitive comparison" their product occupies in a given market as perceived by the target market.

Re-positioning involves changing the identity of a product, relative to the identity of competing products, in the collective minds of the target market.

Product

When a product reaches the maturity stage of the product life cycle a company may choose to operate strategies to extend the life of the product. If the product is predicted to continue to be successful or an upgrade is soon to be released the company can use various methods to keep sales, else the product will be left as is to continue to the decline stage.
Examples of extension strategies are:

· Discounted price
· Increased advertising
· Accessing another market abroad
Another strategy is added value.
This is a widely used extension strategy.

Asset

In business and accounting, assets are economic resources owned by business or company. Anything tangible or intangible that one possesses, usually considered as applicable to the payment of one"s debts is considered an asset. Simplistically stated, assets are things of value that can be readily converted into cash (although cash itself is also considered an asset).

Resources

Human beings are also considered to be Resources because they have the ability to change raw materials into valuable Resources. The term Human Resources can also be defined as the skills, energies, talents, abilities and knowledge that are used for the production of goods or the rendering of services. While taking into account human beings as Resources, the following things have to be kept in mind:

· The size of the population
· The capabilities of the individuals in that population
Many Resources cannot be consumed in their original form. They have to be processed in order to change them into more usable commodities.

Value

A personal and cultural value is a relative ethic value, an assumption upon which implementation can be extrapolated. A value system is a set of consistent values and measures that is soo not true. A principle value is a foundation upon which other values and measures of integrity are based.

Value network

A Value network is a complex set of social and technical resources. Value network s work together via relationships to create social goods (public goods) or economic value.
This value takes the form of knowledge and other intangibles and/or financial value.

Balanced scorecard

The Balanced scorecard (BSC) is a strategic performance management tool for measuring whether the smaller-scale operational activities of a company are aligned with its larger-scale objectives in terms of vision and strategy.

By focusing not only on financial outcomes but also on the operational, marketing and developmental inputs to these, the Balanced scorecard helps provide a more comprehensive view of a business, which in turn helps organizations act in their best long-term interests. This tool is also being used to address business response to climate change and greenhouse gas emissions.

| Strategy map | A strategy map is a visual representation of the strategy of an organization. It illustrates how the organization plans to achieve its mission and vision by means of a linked chain of continuous improvements. |

For a commercial business, the strategy map illustrates the long-term game plan or competitive strategy to achieve increased profitability.

| Value proposition | In the field of marketing, a customer Value proposition consists of the sum total of benefits which a vendor promises that a customer will receive in return for the customer"s associated payment (or other value-transfer.) |

Put simply, the Value proposition is what the customer gets for his money.

Accordingly, a customer can evaluate a company"s value-proposition on two broad dimensions with multiple subsets:

· relative performance: what the customer gets from the vendor relative to a competitor"s offering;
· price: which consists of the payment the customer makes to acquire the product or service; plus the access cost

The vendor-company"s marketing and sales efforts offer a customer Value proposition; the vendor-company"s delivery and customer-service processes then fulfill that value-proposition.

A value-proposition can assist in a firm"s marketing strategy, and may guide a business to target a particular market segment.

| Proposition | This article is about the term proposition in logic and philosophy; for other uses see proposition |

In logic and philosophy, proposition refers to either (a) the "content" or "meaning" of a meaningful declarative sentence or (b) the pattern of symbols, marks, or sounds that make up a meaningful declarative sentence. Propositions in either case are intended to be truth-bearers, that is, they are either true or false.

The existence of propositions in the former sense, as well as the existence of "meanings", is disputed by some philosophers.

Internality	An internality is a term used in behavioral economics to describe those types of behaviors that impose costs on a person in the long-run that are not taken into account when making decisions in the present. Classical Economics discourages government from creating legislation that targets internalities, because it is assumed that the consumer takes these personal costs into account when paying for the good that causes the internality. For example, cigarettes should be taxed because of the negative consumption externalities that they impose, such as second-hand smoke, not because the smoker harms him or herself by smoking.
Business process	A business process or business method is a collection of related, structured activities or tasks that produce a specific service or product (serve a particular goal) for a particular customer or customers. It often can be visualized with a flowchart as a sequence of activities. There are three types of business processes: · Management processes, the processes that govern the operation of a system. Typical management processes include "Corporate Governance" and "Strategic Management". · Operational processes, processes that constitute the core business and create the primary value stream.
Intangible assets	Intangible assets are defined as identifiable non-monetary assets that cannot be seen, touched or physically measured, which are created through time and/or effort and that are identifiable as a separate asset. There are two primary forms of intangibles - legal intangibles (such as trade secrets (e.g., customer lists), copyrights, patents, trademarks, and goodwill) and competitive intangibles (such as knowledge activities (know-how, knowledge), collaboration activities, leverage activities, and structural activities). Legal intangibles are known under the generic term intellectual property and generate legal property rights defensible in a court of law.
Need for Achievement	Need for Achievement (N-Ach) refers to an individual"s desire for significant accomplishment, mastering of skills, control, David McClelland. Need for Achievement is related to the difficulty of tasks people choose to undertake.

Business marketing	Business marketing is the practice of individuals, or organizations, including commercial businesses, governments and institutions, facilitating the sale of their products or services to other companies or organizations that in turn resell them, use them as components in products or services they offer or use them to support their operations. Also known as industrial marketing, Business marketing is also called business-to-Business marketing, or B2B marketing, for short. (Note that while marketing to government entities shares some of the same dynamics of organizational marketing, B2G Marketing is meaningfully different).
International finance	International finance is the branch of economics that studies the dynamics of exchange rates, foreign investment, and how these affect international trade. It also studies international projects, international investments and capital flows, and trade deficits. It includes the study of futures, options and currency swaps.
Need for Achievement	Need for Achievement (N-Ach) refers to an individual"s desire for significant accomplishment, mastering of skills, control, David McClelland. Need for Achievement is related to the difficulty of tasks people choose to undertake.
Business process	A business process or business method is a collection of related, structured activities or tasks that produce a specific service or product (serve a particular goal) for a particular customer or customers. It often can be visualized with a flowchart as a sequence of activities. There are three types of business processes: · Management processes, the processes that govern the operation of a system. Typical management processes include "Corporate Governance" and "Strategic Management". · Operational processes, processes that constitute the core business and create the primary value stream.
Operating costs	Operating costs are the recurring expenses which are related to the operation of a business or to the operation of a device, component, piece of equipment or facility. For a commercial enterprise, Operating costs fall into two broad categories: · fixed costs, which are the same whether the operation is closed or running at 100% capacity · variable costs, which may increase depending on whether more production is done, and how it is done (producing 100 items of product might require 10 days of normal time or take 7 days if overtime is used. It may be more or less expensive to use overtime production depending on whether faster production means the product can be more profitable). Overhead costs for a business are the cost of resources used by an organization just to maintain its existence.

Outsourcing	Outsourcing is subcontracting a service, such as product design or manufacturing, to a third-party company. The decision whether to outsource or to do inhouse is often based upon achieving a lower production cost, making better use of available resources, focussing energy on the core competencies of a particular business, or just making more efficient use of labor, capital, information technology or land resources. It is essentially a division of labour.
Market access	Market access for goods in the WTO means the conditions, tariff and non-tariff measures, agreed by members for the entry of specific goods into their markets. Tariff commitments for goods are set out in each member"s schedules of concessions on goods. The schedules represent commitments not to apply tariffs above the listed rates -- these rates are "bound".
Role	A role or a social role is a set of connected behaviors, rights and obligations as conceptualized by actors in a social situation. It is an expected behavior in a given individual social status and social position. It is vital to both functionalist and interactionist understandings of society.
Customer service	Customer service is the provision of service to customers before, during and after a purchase. According to Jamier L. Scott. (2002), "Customer service is a series of activities designed to enhance the level of customer satisfaction - that is, the feeling that a product or service has met the customer expectation." Its importance varies by product, industry and customer; defective or broken merchandise can be exchanged/swapped, often only with a receipt and within a specified time frame.
Risk	Risk is a concept that denotes the precise probability of specific eventualities. Technically, the notion of Risk is independent from the notion of value and, as such, eventualities may have both beneficial and adverse consequences. However, in general usage the convention is to focus only on potential negative impact to some characteristic of value that may arise from a future event.
Mind control	Mind control (also referred to as brainwashing, coercive persuasion, and thought reform) refers to a broad range of psychological tactics thought to subvert an individual"s control of his or her own thinking, behavior, emotions).
Dangerous goods	Dangerous goods,), are solids, liquids, other living organisms, property, or the environment. They are often subject to chemical regulations. dangerous goods include materials that are radioactive, flammable, explosive or corrosive, oxidizers or asphyxiants, biohazardous, toxic, pathogen or allergen substances and organisms.
International trade	International trade is exchange of capital, goods, and services across international borders or territories. In most countries, it represents a significant share of gross domestic product (GDP). While International trade has been present throughout much of history , its economic, social, and political importance has been on the rise in recent centuries.
Contract	In common-law systems, the five key requirements for the creation of a Contract are: 1. offer and acceptance (agreement) 2. consideration 3. an intention to create legal relations 4. legal capacity 5. formalities

In civil-law systems, the concept of consideration is not central. In addition, for some Contracts formalities must be complied with under what is sometimes called a statute of frauds.

One of the most famous cases on forming a Contract is Carlill v. Carbolic Smoke Ball Company, decided in nineteenth-century England.

Contract manufacturing	A contract manufacturer is a firm that manufactures components or products for another "hiring" firm. It is a form of outsourcing. The practice of utilizing Contract manufacturing relies on the manufacturer"s ability to drive down the cost of production through economies of scale.
Management contract	A Management contract is an arrangement under which operational control of an enterprise is vested by contract in a separate enterprise which performs the necessary managerial functions in return for a fee. Management contracts involve not just selling a method of doing things (as with franchising or licensing) but involves actually doing them. A Management contract can involve a wide range of functions, such as technical operation of a production facility, management of personnel, accounting, marketing services and training.
Joint venture	Some countries, such as the People"s Republic of China and to some extent India, require foreign companies to form Joint ventures with domestic firms in order to enter a market. This requirement often forces technology transfers and managerial control to the domestic partner. In addition, Joint ventures are practiced by a Joint venture broker, who are people that often put together the two parties that participate in a Joint venture.
Xerox Corporation	Xerox Corporation is a global document management company which manufactures and sells a range of color and black-and-white printers, multifunction systems, photo copiers, digital production printing presses, and related consulting services and supplies. Xerox is headquartered in Norwalk, Connecticut , though its largest population of employees is based in and around Rochester, New York, the area in which the company was founded. The Xerox 914 was the first one-piece plain paper photocopier, and sold in the thousands. Xerox was founded in 1906 in Rochester, New York as "The Haloid Company", which originally manufactured photographic paper and equipment.
Global strategy	Global strategy as defined in business terms is an organization"s strategic guide to globalization. A sound global strategy should address these questions: what must be (versus what is) the extent of market presence in the world"s major markets? How to build the necessary global presence? What must be (versus what is) the optimal locations around the world for the various value chain activities? How to run global presence into global competitive advantage? Academic research on global strategy came of age during the 1980s, including work by Michael Porter and Christopher Bartlett ' Sumantra Ghoshal. Among the forces perceived to bring about the globalization of competition were convergence in economic systems and technological change, especially in information technology, that facilitated and required the coordination of a multinational firm"s strategy on a worldwide scale.

Industries	An industry is the manufacturing of a good or service within a category. Although industry is a broad term for any kind of economic production, in economics and urban planning industry is a synonym for the secondary sector, which is a type of economic activity involved in the manufacturing of raw materials into goods and products.
	There are four key industrial economic sectors: the primary sector, largely raw material extraction industries such as mining and farming; the secondary sector, involving refining, construction, and manufacturing; the tertiary sector, which deals with services and distribution of manufactured goods; and the quaternary sector, a relatively new type of knowledge industry focusing on technological research, design and development such as computer programming, and biochemistry.
Competition	Co-operative competition is based upon promoting mutual survival - "everyone wins". Adam Smith"s "invisible hand" is a process where individuals compete to improve their level of happiness but compete in a cooperative manner through peaceful exchange and without violating other people. Cooperative competition focuses individuals/groups/organisms against the environment.
Consumer	Consumer is a broad label for any individuals or households that use goods and services generated within the economy. The concept of a Consumer is used in different contexts, so that the usage and significance of the term may vary.
	Typically when business people and economists talk of Consumers they are talking about person as Consumer, an aggregated commodity item with little individuality other than that expressed in the buy/not-buy decision.
Product	When a product reaches the maturity stage of the product life cycle a company may choose to operate strategies to extend the life of the product. If the product is predicted to continue to be successful or an upgrade is soon to be released the company can use various methods to keep sales, else the product will be left as is to continue to the decline stage.
	Examples of extension strategies are:
	· Discounted price · Increased advertising · Accessing another market abroad Another strategy is added value. This is a widely used extension strategy.
Emerging	Emerging is the title of the only album by the Phil Keaggy Band, released in 1977 on NewSong Records. The album was re-released on CD in 2000 as Reemerging with a different track listing, including four newly recorded songs by the original band members.
	All songs written by Phil Keaggy, unless otherwise noted.

· "Theme" (Phil Madeira) - 1:25 (instrumental)
· "Where Is My Maker?" - 2:25
· "Another Try" - 4:55
· "Ryan"s Song" (inspired by a poem by Bill Clarke) - 3:09
· "Struck By The Love" (Madeira) - 5:43 (lead vocal: Phil Madeira)

· "Turned On The Light" - 4:57
· "Sorry" - 4:09
· "Take A Look Around" - 5:16
· "Gentle Eyes" - 5:29

All songs written by Phil Keaggy, unless otherwise noted.

· "Theme"
· "Where Is My Maker?"
· "Another Try"
· "Ryan"s Song"
· "Struck By The Love"
· "Turned On The Light"
· "Sorry"
· "Take A Look Around"
· "My Auburn Lady" - 4:26
· "Mighty Lord" (Madeira) - 4:43 (lead vocal: Phil Madeira)
· "You"re My Hero" (Andersen/Keaggy) - 4:04 (lead vocal: Terry Andersen)
· "Amelia Earhart"s Last Flight" (McEnery) - 3:17 (lead vocal: Dan Cunningham)

· Dan Cunningham - bass, vocals (CD reissue only)
· Lynn Nichols - vocals, electric guitar, acoustic guitar (lead on "Struck By The Love"), classical guitar.
· Phil Keaggy - vocals, lead electric and acoustic guitar
· Phil Madeira - vocals, piano, Hammond Organ, Fender Rhodes, Micro ' Polymoog synths
· Terry Andersen - drums, vocals (CD reissue only)

· Karl Fruh - Cello on "Another Try"
· Ray Papai - Sax on "Sorry"

· Produced by Peter K. Hopper with Phil Keaggy.
· Engineered ' Mixed by Gary Hedden.

| Emerging markets | The term emerging markets is used to describe a nation"s social or business activity in the process of rapid growth and industrialization. Currently, there are approximately 28 emerging markets in the world, with the economies of India and China considered to be by far the two largest. According to The Economist many people find the term dated, but a new term has yet to gain much traction. |

Risk management	Risk management is activity directed towards the assessing, mitigating (to an acceptable level) and monitoring of risks. In some cases the acceptable risk may be near zero. Risks can come from accidents, natural causes and disasters as well as deliberate attacks from an adversary.
Schwinn	The Schwinn Bicycle Company was founded by Ignaz Schwinn in Chicago in 1895 and became the dominant manufacturer of American bicycles through most of the 20th century. The company"s rise and fall in fortunes over its lifetime has been widely used to illustrate the issues faced by entrenched companies in a dynamic and changing marketing environment. Ignaz Schwinn was born in Hardheim, Germany in 1860 and worked on two-wheeled ancestors of the modern bicycle that appeared in 19th century Europe.
Case study	A case study is one of several ways of doing research whether it is social science related or even socially related. It is an intensive study of a single group, incident, or community. Other ways include experiments, surveys, or analysis of archival information .

Product	When a product reaches the maturity stage of the product life cycle a company may choose to operate strategies to extend the life of the product. If the product is predicted to continue to be successful or an upgrade is soon to be released the company can use various methods to keep sales, else the product will be left as is to continue to the decline stage. Examples of extension strategies are: · Discounted price · Increased advertising · Accessing another market abroad Another strategy is added value. This is a widely used extension strategy.
Brand equity	Brand equity refers to the marketing effects or outcomes that accrue to a product with its brand name compared with those that would accrue if the same product did not have the brand name . And, at the root of these marketing effects is consumers" knowledge. In other words, consumers" knowledge about a brand makes manufacturers/advertisers respond differently or adopt appropriately adept measures for the marketing of the brand .
Defined	In mathematics, Defined and unDefined are used to explain whether or not expressions have meaningful, sensible, and unambiguous values. Whether an expression has a meaningful value depends on the context of the expression. For example the value of 4 − 5 is unDefined if a positive integer result is required.
Inventory	Inventory is a list for goods and materials, held available in stock by a business. It is also used for a list of the contents of a household and for a list for testamentary purposes of the possessions of someone who has died. In accounting Inventory is considered an asset.
Quality	Quality in business, engineering and manufacturing has a pragmatic interpretation as the non-inferiority or superiority of something. Quality is a perceptual, conditional and somewhat subjective attribute and may be understood differently by different people. Consumers may focus on the specification Quality of a product/service, or how it compares to competitors in the marketplace.
Customer profitability	Customer profitability is the difference between the revenues earned from and the costs associated with the customer relationship in a specified period. According to Philip Kotler,"a profitable customer is a person, household or a company that overtime, yields a revenue stream that exceeds by an acceptable amount the company"s cost stream of attracting, selling and servicing the customer" Although Customer profitability is nothing more than the result of applying the business concept of profit to a customer relationship, measuring the profitability of a firm"s customers or customer groups can often deliver useful business insights. Quite often a very small percentage of the firm"s best customers will account for a large portion of firm profit.
Standard	A technical standard is an established norm or requirement. It is usually a formal document that establishes uniform engineering or technical criteria, methods, processes and practices.

A technical standard can also be a controlled artifact or similar formal means used for calibration.

Supplier	A supply chain is the system of organizations, people, technology, activities, information and resources involved in moving a product or service from Supplier to customer. Supply chain activities transform natural resources, raw materials and components into a finished product that is delivered to the end customer. In sophisticated supply chain systems, used products may re-enter the supply chain at any point where residual value is recyclable.
Value	A personal and cultural value is a relative ethic value, an assumption upon which implementation can be extrapolated. A value system is a set of consistent values and measures that is soo not true. A principle value is a foundation upon which other values and measures of integrity are based.
Product line	There are many important decisions about product and service development and marketing. In the process of product development and marketing we should focus on strategic decisions about product attributes, product branding, product packaging, product labeling and product support services. But product strategy also calls for building a Product line.
Consideration	Consideration is the legal concept of value in connection with contracts. It is anything of value in the common sense, promised to another when making a contract. It can take the form of money, physical objects, services, promised actions, or even abstinence from a future action.
Pricing	Pricing is a fundamental aspect of financial modelling, and is one of the four Ps of the marketing mix. The other three aspects are product, promotion, and place. It is also a key variable in microeconomic price allocation theory.
Product support	Product support is a service provided by many retailers of various products, primarily electronics, that provides the end-user with a resource for information regarding the product, and help if the product should malfunction. Product support can be found in most manuals for products in the form of a phone number, website address, or physical location. The Internet has allowed for a new form of Product support to develop.
Strategy	A Strategy is a plan of action designed to achieve a particular goal. Strategy is different from tactics. In military terms, tactics is concerned with the conduct of an engagement while Strategy is concerned with how different engagements are linked.
Stereotype	A stereotype is a commonly held public belief about specific social groups, based on some prior assumptions.
Product market	Product market is a mechanism that allows people easily to buy and sell products. Services are often included in the scope of the term. Product market regulation is an economic term that describes restrictions in the market.

Restrictive	In semantics, a modifier is said to be restrictive (or defining) if it restricts the reference of its head. For example, in "the red car is fancier than the blue one", red and blue are restrictive, because they restrict which cars car and one are referring to. ("The car is fancier than the one" would make little sense).
Opportunities	"opportunities (Let"s Make Lots of Money)" is a song by UK synthpop duo Pet Shop Boys, released as a single in 1985 and then in 1986, gaining greater popularity in both the UK and U.S. with its second release.
	Written as a satire of Thatcherism and its embodiment in conspicuous consumption and yuppies in the United Kingdom during the 1980s, the song"s indirect attack on its subject matter has come to exemplify the Pet Shop Boys as ironists in their songwriting.
	The song was written during the Pet Shop Boys" formative years, in 1983. According to Neil Tennant, the main lyrical concept came while in a recording studio in Camden Town when Chris Lowe asked him to make up a lyric based around the line "Let"s make lots of money".
Positioning	In marketing, positioning has come to mean the process by which marketers try to create an image or identity in the minds of their target market for its product, brand, or organization. It is the "relative competitive comparison" their product occupies in a given market as perceived by the target market. Re-positioning involves changing the identity of a product, relative to the identity of competing products, in the collective minds of the target market.
Technology	Technology is a broad concept that deals with an animal species" usage and knowledge of tools and crafts, and how it affects an animal species" ability to control and adapt to its environment. Technology is a term with origins in the Greek "technologia", "τεχνολογÎ¯α" -- "techne", "τÎ̄χνη" and "logia", "λογÎ¯α" ("saying".) However, a strict definition is elusive; "Technology" can refer to material objects of use to humanity, such as machines, hardware or utensils, but can also encompass broader themes, including systems, methods of organization, and techniques.
Discontinuity	Continuous functions are of utmost importance in mathematics and applications. However, not all functions are continuous. If a function is not continuous at a point in its domain, one says that it has a discontinuity there.
Need for Achievement	Need for Achievement (N-Ach) refers to an individual"s desire for significant accomplishment, mastering of skills, control, David McClelland.
	Need for Achievement is related to the difficulty of tasks people choose to undertake.
Note	In music, the term Note has two primary meanings:
	· a sign used in musical notation to represent the relative duration and pitch of a sound; · a pitched sound itself.
	Notes are the "atoms" of much Western music: discretizations of musical phenomena that facilitate performance, comprehension, and analysis .

85

The term "Note" can be used in both generic and specific senses: one might say either "the piece Happy Birthday to You begins with two Notes having the same pitch," or "the piece begins with two repetitions of the same Note." In the former case, one uses "Note" to refer to a specific musical event; in the latter, one uses the term to refer to a class of events sharing the same pitch.

Internet marketing

Internet marketing, also referred to as i-marketing, web marketing, online marketing, is the marketing of products, or, services over the Internet.

The Internet has brought media to a global audience. The interactive nature of Internet marketing, both, in terms of providing instant response and eliciting responses, is a unique quality of the medium.

86

Product

When a product reaches the maturity stage of the product life cycle a company may choose to operate strategies to extend the life of the product. If the product is predicted to continue to be successful or an upgrade is soon to be released the company can use various methods to keep sales, else the product will be left as is to continue to the decline stage.

Examples of extension strategies are:

· Discounted price
· Increased advertising
· Accessing another market abroad
Another strategy is added value.
This is a widely used extension strategy.

Product development

In business and engineering, new Product development (NPD) is the term used to describe the complete process of bringing a new product or service to market. There are two parallel paths involved in the NPD process: one involves the idea generation, product design, and detail engineering; the other involves market research and marketing analysis. Companies typically see new Product development as the first stage in generating and commercializing new products within the overall strategic process of product life cycle management used to maintain or grow their market share.

· Idea Generation is often called the "fuzzy front end" of the NPD process

· Ideas for new products can be obtained from basic research using a SWOT analysis (Strengths, Weaknesses, Opportunities ' Threats), Market and consumer trends, company"s R'D department, competitors, focus groups, employees, salespeople, corporate spies, trade shows, or Ethnographic discovery methods (searching for user patterns and habits) may also be used to get an insight into new product lines or product features.
· Idea Generation or Brainstorming of new product, service, or store concepts - idea generation techniques can begin when you have done your OPPORTUNITY ANALYSIS to support your ideas in the Idea Screening Phase (shown in the next development step).
· Idea Screening

· The object is to eliminate unsound concepts prior to devoting resources to them.
· The screeners must ask at least three questions:

· Will the customer in the target market benefit from the product?
· What is the size and growth forecasts of the market segment/target market?
· What is the current or expected competitive pressure for the product idea?
· What are the industry sales and market trends the product idea is based on?
· Is it technically feasible to manufacture the product?
· Will the product be profitable when manufactured and delivered to the customer at the target price?
· Concept Development and Testing

· Develop the marketing and engineering details

· Who is the target market and who is the decision maker in the purchasing process?

· What product features must the product incorporate?

· What benefits will the product provide?

· How will consumers react to the product?

· How will the product be produced most cost effectively?

· Prove feasibility through virtual computer aided rendering, and rapid prototyping

· What will it cost to produce it?

· Testing the Concept by asking a sample of prospective customers what they think of the idea.

Asset	In business and accounting, assets are economic resources owned by business or company. Anything tangible or intangible that one possesses, usually considered as applicable to the payment of one"s debts is considered an asset. Simplistically stated, assets are things of value that can be readily converted into cash (although cash itself is also considered an asset).
BlackBerry	BlackBerry is a line of wireless handheld devices that was introduced in 1999 as a two-way pager. In 2002, the more commonly known smartphone BlackBerry was released, which supports push e-mail, mobile telephone, text messaging, internet faxing, web browsing and other wireless information services. It is an example of a convergent device.
Data migration	Data migration is the process of transferring data between storage types, formats, freeing up human resources from tedious tasks. It is required when organizations or individuals change computer systems or upgrade to new systems, or when systems merge (such as when the organizations that use them undergo a merger/takeover).
Inventory	Inventory is a list for goods and materials, held available in stock by a business. It is also used for a list of the contents of a household and for a list for testamentary purposes of the possessions of someone who has died. In accounting Inventory is considered an asset.
Determinant	In algebra, the determinant is a special number associated to any square matrix, that is to say, a rectangular array of numbers where the (finite) number of rows and columns are equal. The fundamental geometric meaning of a determinant is a scale factor for measure when the matrix is regarded as a linear transformation. Thus a 2 × 2 matrix with determinant 2 when applied to a set of points with finite area will transform those points into a set with twice the area.
Dangerous goods	Dangerous goods,), are solids, liquids, other living organisms, property, or the environment. They are often subject to chemical regulations. dangerous goods include materials that are radioactive, flammable, explosive or corrosive, oxidizers or asphyxiants, biohazardous, toxic, pathogen or allergen substances and organisms.
Entrepreneurship	For Frank H. Knight (1921) and Peter Drucker (1970) entrepreneurship is about taking risk. The behavior of the entrepreneur reflects a kind of person willing to put his or her career and financial security on the line and take risks in the name of an idea, spending much time as well as capital on an uncertain venture. Knight classified three types of uncertainty.

· Risk, which is measurable statistically .

· Ambiguity, which is hard to measure statistically .

· True Uncertainty or Knightian Uncertainty, which is impossible to estimate or predict statistically .

Xerox Corporation	Xerox Corporation is a global document management company which manufactures and sells a range of color and black-and-white printers, multifunction systems, photo copiers, digital production printing presses, and related consulting services and supplies. Xerox is headquartered in Norwalk, Connecticut , though its largest population of employees is based in and around Rochester, New York, the area in which the company was founded. The Xerox 914 was the first one-piece plain paper photocopier, and sold in the thousands. Xerox was founded in 1906 in Rochester, New York as "The Haloid Company", which originally manufactured photographic paper and equipment.
Technology	Technology is a broad concept that deals with an animal species" usage and knowledge of tools and crafts, and how it affects an animal species" ability to control and adapt to its environment. Technology is a term with origins in the Greek "technologia", "τεχνολογÎ¯α" -- "techne", "τÎ̄χνη" and "logia", "λογÎ¯α" ("saying".) However, a strict definition is elusive; "Technology" can refer to material objects of use to humanity, such as machines, hardware or utensils, but can also encompass broader themes, including systems, methods of organization, and techniques.
Disruptive innovation	Disruptive technology and disruptive innovation are terms used in business and technology literature to describe innovations that improve a product or service in ways that the market does not expect, typically by being lower priced or designed for a different set of consumers. disruptive innovations can be broadly classified into low-end and new-market disruptive innovations. A new-market disruptive innovation is often aimed at non-consumption (i.e., consumers who would not have used the products already on the market), whereas a lower-end disruptive innovation is aimed at mainstream customers for whom price is more important than quality.
Strategy	A Strategy is a plan of action designed to achieve a particular goal. Strategy is different from tactics. In military terms, tactics is concerned with the conduct of an engagement while Strategy is concerned with how different engagements are linked.
Sale	A sale is the pinnacle activity involved in selling products or services in return for money or other compensation. It is an act of completion of a commercial activity. A sale is completed by the seller, the owner of the goods.
Real-time	In computer science, real-time computing (RTC), is the study of hardware and software systems that are subject to a "real-time constraint"--i.e., operational deadlines from event to system response. By contrast, a non-real-time system is one for which there is no deadline, even if fast response or high performance is desired or preferred. The needs of real-time software are often addressed in the context of real-time operating systems, and synchronous programming languages, which provide frameworks on which to build real-time application software.

Marketing	marketing is a "social and managerial process by which individuals and groups obtain what they need and want through creating and exchanging products and values with others." It is an integrated process through which companies create value for customers and build strong customer relationships in order to capture value from customers in return.
	marketing is used to create the customer, to keep the customer and to satisfy the customer. With the customer as the focus of its activities, it can be concluded that marketing management is one of the major components of business management.
New product development	In business and engineering, new product development is the term used to describe the complete process of bringing a new product or service to market. There are two parallel paths involved in the new product development process: one involves the idea generation, product design, and detail engineering; the other involves market research and marketing analysis. Companies typically see new product development as the first stage in generating and commercializing new products within the overall strategic process of product life cycle management used to maintain or grow their market share.
	· Idea Generation is often called the "fuzzy front end" of the new product development process
	· Ideas for new products can be obtained from basic research using a SWOT analysis (Strengths, Weaknesses, Opportunities ' Threats), Market and consumer trends, company"s R'D department, competitors, focus groups, employees, salespeople, corporate spies, trade shows, or Ethnographic discovery methods (searching for user patterns and habits) may also be used to get an insight into new product lines or product features.
	· Idea Generation or Brainstorming of new product, service, or store concepts - idea generation techniques can begin when you have done your OPPORTUNITY ANALYSIS to support your ideas in the Idea Screening Phase (shown in the next development step).
	· Idea Screening
	· The object is to eliminate unsound concepts prior to devoting resources to them.
	· The screeners must ask at least three questions:
	· Will the customer in the target market benefit from the product?
	· What is the size and growth forecasts of the market segment/target market?
	· What is the current or expected competitive pressure for the product idea?
	· What are the industry sales and market trends the product idea is based on?
	· Is it technically feasible to manufacture the product?
	· Will the product be profitable when manufactured and delivered to the customer at the target price?
	· Concept Development and Testing
	· Develop the marketing and engineering details

· Who is the target market and who is the decision maker in the purchasing process?
· What product features must the product incorporate?
· What benefits will the product provide?
· How will consumers react to the product?
· How will the product be produced most cost effectively?
· Prove feasibility through virtual computer aided rendering, and rapid prototyping
· What will it cost to produce it?
· Testing the Concept by asking a sample of prospective customers what they think of the idea.

Resources	Human beings are also considered to be Resources because they have the ability to change raw materials into valuable Resources. The term Human Resources can also be defined as the skills, energies, talents, abilities and knowledge that are used for the production of goods or the rendering of services. While taking into account human beings as Resources, the following things have to be kept in mind: · The size of the population · The capabilities of the individuals in that population Many Resources cannot be consumed in their original form. They have to be processed in order to change them into more usable commodities.
Co-operative competition	Co-operative competition is based upon promoting mutual survival - "everyone wins". Adam Smith"s "invisible hand" is a process where individuals compete to improve their level of happiness but compete in a cooperative manner through peaceful exchange and without violating other people. Cooperative competition focuses individuals/groups/organisms against the environment.
Product design	Product design can be defined as the idea generation, concept development, testing and manufacturing or implementation of a physical object or service. Product designers conceptualize and evaluate ideas, making them tangible through products in a more systematic approach. The role of a Product designer encompasses many characteristics of the marketing manager, product manager, industrial designer and design engineer.
Procurement	Procurement is the acquisition of goods and/or services at the best possible total cost of ownership, in the right quality and quantity, at the right time, in the right place and from the right source for the direct benefit or use of corporations, individuals, generally via a contract, or it can be the same way selection for human resource Simple Procurement may involve nothing more than repeat purchasing. Complex Procurement could involve finding long term partners - or even "co-destiny" suppliers that might fundamentally commit one organization to another. Almost all purchasing decisions include factors such as delivery and handling, marginal benefit, and price fluctuations.
Synergy	Synergy is the term used to describe a situation where different entities cooperate advantageously for a final outcome. Simply defined, it means that the whole is greater than the sum of its parts. The essence of Synergy is to value differences.

Customer experience	Customer experience is the sum of all experiences a customer has with a supplier of goods or services, over the duration of their relationship with that supplier. It can also be used to mean an individual experience over one transaction; the distinction is usually clear in context.
	The concept of Customer experience was first introduced by Pine and Gilmore in their 1998 Harvard Business Review article.
Best practice	A best practice is a technique, method, process, activity, incentive or reward that is believed to be more effective at delivering a particular outcome than any other technique, method, process, etc. The idea is that with proper processes, checks, and testing, a desired outcome can be delivered with fewer problems and unforeseen complications. best practices can also be defined as the most efficient (least amount of effort) and effective (best results) way of accomplishing a task, based on repeatable procedures that have proven themselves over time for large numbers of people.
Relationship management	Customer Relationship management (C Relationship management) consists of the processes a company uses to track and organize its contacts with its current and prospective customers. C Relationship management software is used to support these processes; information about customers and customer interactions can be entered, stored and accessed by employees in different company departments. Typical C Relationship management goals are to improve services provided to customers, and to use customer contact information for targeted marketing.
Touchpoint	Touchpoint (also touch point, contact point, customer contact, point of contact, brand Touchpoint, and customer Touchpoint) is the interface
	· of a product, · a service or · a brand with customers, non-customers, employees and other stakeholders - before, during and after a transaction respectively a purchase. This applies for business-to-business- as well as business-to-consumer-markets.
	A ROI oriented management aims at the augmentation and the optimisation of the impact and the cost-benefit ratio of the internal and external processes.
Solution	In chemistry, a solution is a homogeneous mixture composed of two or more substances. In such a mixture, a solute is dissolved in another substance, known as a solvent. Gases may dissolve in liquids, for example, carbon dioxide or oxygen in water.
Celebrity branding	Celebrity branding is a type of branding, in which a celebrity uses his or her status in society to promote a product, service or charity. Celebrity branding can take several different forms, from a celebrity simply appearing in advertisements for a product, service or charity, to a celebrity attending PR events, creating his or her own line of products or services, and/or using his or her name as a brand. The most popular forms of celebrity brand lines are for clothing and fragrances.
Consumer	Consumer is a broad label for any individuals or households that use goods and services generated within the economy. The concept of a Consumer is used in different contexts, so that the usage and significance of the term may vary.

Typically when business people and economists talk of Consumers they are talking about person as Consumer, an aggregated commodity item with little individuality other than that expressed in the buy/not-buy decision.

Product	When a product reaches the maturity stage of the product life cycle a company may choose to operate strategies to extend the life of the product. If the product is predicted to continue to be successful or an upgrade is soon to be released the company can use various methods to keep sales, else the product will be left as is to continue to the decline stage. Examples of extension strategies are: · Discounted price · Increased advertising · Accessing another market abroad Another strategy is added value. This is a widely used extension strategy.
Marketing	marketing is a "social and managerial process by which individuals and groups obtain what they need and want through creating and exchanging products and values with others." It is an integrated process through which companies create value for customers and build strong customer relationships in order to capture value from customers in return. marketing is used to create the customer, to keep the customer and to satisfy the customer. With the customer as the focus of its activities, it can be concluded that marketing management is one of the major components of business management.
Inventory	Inventory is a list for goods and materials, held available in stock by a business. It is also used for a list of the contents of a household and for a list for testamentary purposes of the possessions of someone who has died. In accounting Inventory is considered an asset.
Goods and services	In economics, economic output is divided into physical goods and intangible services. Consumption of goods and services is assumed to produce utility. It is often used when referring to a goods and services Tax.
Services Marketing	Services marketing is marketing based on relationship and value. It may be used to market a service or a product. Marketing a service-base business is different from marketing a goods-base business.
Real-time	In computer science, real-time computing (RTC), is the study of hardware and software systems that are subject to a "real-time constraint"--i.e., operational deadlines from event to system response. By contrast, a non-real-time system is one for which there is no deadline, even if fast response or high performance is desired or preferred. The needs of real-time software are often addressed in the context of real-time operating systems, and synchronous programming languages, which provide frameworks on which to build real-time application software.

Quality	Quality in business, engineering and manufacturing has a pragmatic interpretation as the non-inferiority or superiority of something. Quality is a perceptual, conditional and somewhat subjective attribute and may be understood differently by different people. Consumers may focus on the specification Quality of a product/service, or how it compares to competitors in the marketplace.
Customer satisfaction	Customer satisfaction, a business term, is a measure of how products and services supplied by a company meet or surpass customer expectation. It is seen as a key performance indicator within business and is part of the four perspectives of a Balanced Scorecard. In a competitive marketplace where businesses compete for customers, Customer satisfaction is seen as a key differentiator and increasingly has become a key element of business strategy.
Marketing mix	The four main fields of the marketing mix. The marketing mix is generally accepted as the use and specification of the "four Ps" describing the strategy position of a product in the marketplace. The "marketing mix" is a set of controllable, tactical marketing tools that work together to achieve company"s objectives. One version of the marketing mix originated in 1948 when James Culliton said that a marketing decision should be a result of something similar to a recipe.
Pricing	Pricing is a fundamental aspect of financial modelling, and is one of the four Ps of the marketing mix. The other three aspects are product, promotion, and place. It is also a key variable in microeconomic price allocation theory.
Strategic alliance	A strategic alliance is a formal relationship between two or more parties to pursue a set of agreed upon goals or to meet a critical business need while remaining independent organizations. Partners may provide the strategic alliance with resources such as products, distribution channels, manufacturing capability, project funding, capital equipment, knowledge, expertise, or intellectual property. The alliance is a cooperation or collaboration which aims for a synergy where each partner hopes that the benefits from the alliance will be greater than those from individual efforts.
Customer profitability	Customer profitability is the difference between the revenues earned from and the costs associated with the customer relationship in a specified period. According to Philip Kotler,"a profitable customer is a person, household or a company that overtime, yields a revenue stream that exceeds by an acceptable amount the company"s cost stream of attracting, selling and servicing the customer" Although Customer profitability is nothing more than the result of applying the business concept of profit to a customer relationship, measuring the profitability of a firm"s customers or customer groups can often deliver useful business insights. Quite often a very small percentage of the firm"s best customers will account for a large portion of firm profit.
Promotion	Promotion involves disseminating information about a product, product line, brand, or company. It is one of the four key aspects of the marketing mix. (The other three elements are product marketing, pricing, and distribution). P>Promotion is generally sub-divided into two parts:

· Above the line Promotion: Promotion in the media (e.g. TV, radio, newspapers, Internet and Mobile Phones) in which the advertiser pays an advertising agency to place the ad

· Below the line Promotion: All other Promotion. Much of this is intended to be subtle enough for the consumer to be unaware that Promotion is taking place. E.g. sponsorship, product placement, endorsements, sales Promotion, merchandising, direct mail, personal selling, public relations, trade shows

Sale	A sale is the pinnacle activity involved in selling products or services in return for money or other compensation. It is an act of completion of a commercial activity.
	A sale is completed by the seller, the owner of the goods.
Distribution	Distribution (or place) is one of the four elements of marketing mix. An organization or set of organizations (go-betweens) involved in the process of making a product or service available for use or consumption by a consumer or business user.
	The other three parts of the marketing mix are product, pricing, and promotion.
Business marketing	Business marketing is the practice of individuals, or organizations, including commercial businesses, governments and institutions, facilitating the sale of their products or services to other companies or organizations that in turn resell them, use them as components in products or services they offer or use them to support their operations. Also known as industrial marketing, Business marketing is also called business-to-Business marketing, or B2B marketing, for short. (Note that while marketing to government entities shares some of the same dynamics of organizational marketing, B2G Marketing is meaningfully different).

Business marketing	Business marketing is the practice of individuals, or organizations, including commercial businesses, governments and institutions, facilitating the sale of their products or services to other companies or organizations that in turn resell them, use them as components in products or services they offer or use them to support their operations. Also known as industrial marketing, Business marketing is also called business-to-Business marketing, or B2B marketing, for short. (Note that while marketing to government entities shares some of the same dynamics of organizational marketing, B2G Marketing is meaningfully different).
Distribution	Distribution (or place) is one of the four elements of marketing mix. An organization or set of organizations (go-betweens) involved in the process of making a product or service available for use or consumption by a consumer or business user. The other three parts of the marketing mix are product, pricing, and promotion.
Best practice	A best practice is a technique, method, process, activity, incentive or reward that is believed to be more effective at delivering a particular outcome than any other technique, method, process, etc. The idea is that with proper processes, checks, and testing, a desired outcome can be delivered with fewer problems and unforeseen complications. best practices can also be defined as the most efficient (least amount of effort) and effective (best results) way of accomplishing a task, based on repeatable procedures that have proven themselves over time for large numbers of people.
Collaboration	Collaboration is a recursive process where two or more people or organizations work together in an intersection of common goals -- for example, an intellectual endeavor that is creative in nature--by sharing knowledge, learning and building consensus. Most Collaboration requires leadership, although the form of leadership can be social within a decentralized and egalitarian group. In particular, teams that work collaboratively can obtain greater resources, recognition and reward when facing competition for finite resources.Collaboration is also present in opposing goals exhibiting the notion of adversarial Collaboration, though this is not a common case for using the term.
Relationship management	Customer Relationship management (C Relationship management) consists of the processes a company uses to track and organize its contacts with its current and prospective customers. C Relationship management software is used to support these processes; information about customers and customer interactions can be entered, stored and accessed by employees in different company departments. Typical C Relationship management goals are to improve services provided to customers, and to use customer contact information for targeted marketing.
Dangerous goods	Dangerous goods,), are solids, liquids, other living organisms, property, or the environment. They are often subject to chemical regulations. dangerous goods include materials that are radioactive, flammable, explosive or corrosive, oxidizers or asphyxiants, biohazardous, toxic, pathogen or allergen substances and organisms.
Point	In typography, a point is the smallest unit of measure, being a subdivision of the larger pica. It is commonly abbreviated as pt. The traditional printer"s point, from the era of hot metal typesetting and presswork, varied between 0.18 and 0.4 mm depending on various definitions of the foot.

Today, the traditional point has been supplanted by the desktop publishing point (also called the PostScript point), which has been rounded to an even 72 points to the inch (1 point = $\frac{127}{360}$ mm ≈ 0.353 mm).

Solution	In chemistry, a solution is a homogeneous mixture composed of two or more substances. In such a mixture, a solute is dissolved in another substance, known as a solvent. Gases may dissolve in liquids, for example, carbon dioxide or oxygen in water.
Strategy	A Strategy is a plan of action designed to achieve a particular goal. Strategy is different from tactics. In military terms, tactics is concerned with the conduct of an engagement while Strategy is concerned with how different engagements are linked.
Case study	A case study is one of several ways of doing research whether it is social science related or even socially related. It is an intensive study of a single group, incident, or community. Other ways include experiments, surveys, or analysis of archival information .
Sale	A sale is the pinnacle activity involved in selling products or services in return for money or other compensation. It is an act of completion of a commercial activity. A sale is completed by the seller, the owner of the goods.
Expert opinion	An expert witness or professional witness is a witness, who by virtue of education, training, skill, is believed to have knowledge in a particular subject beyond that of the average person, sufficient that others may officially rely upon the witness"s specialized (scientific, technical or other) opinion about an evidence or fact issue within the scope of their expertise, referred to as the Expert opinion, as an assistance to the fact-finder. Expert witnesses may also deliver expert evidence about facts from the domain of their expertise. At times, their testimony may be rebutted with a learned treatise, sometimes to the detriment of their reputations.
Restrictive	In semantics, a modifier is said to be restrictive (or defining) if it restricts the reference of its head. For example, in "the red car is fancier than the blue one", red and blue are restrictive, because they restrict which cars car and one are referring to. ("The car is fancier than the one" would make little sense).
Balanced scorecard	The Balanced scorecard (BSC) is a strategic performance management tool for measuring whether the smaller-scale operational activities of a company are aligned with its larger-scale objectives in terms of vision and strategy. By focusing not only on financial outcomes but also on the operational, marketing and developmental inputs to these, the Balanced scorecard helps provide a more comprehensive view of a business, which in turn helps organizations act in their best long-term interests. This tool is also being used to address business response to climate change and greenhouse gas emissions.

Benchmarking	Benchmarking is the process of comparing the business processes and performance metrics including cost, cycle time, productivity, Benchmarking provides a snapshot of the performance of your business and helps you understand where you are in relation to a particular standard. The result is often a business case and "Burning Platform" for making changes in order to make improvements.
Co-operative competition	Co-operative competition is based upon promoting mutual survival - "everyone wins". Adam Smith"s "invisible hand" is a process where individuals compete to improve their level of happiness but compete in a cooperative manner through peaceful exchange and without violating other people. Cooperative competition focuses individuals/groups/organisms against the environment.
Disintermediation	In economics, Disintermediation is the removal of intermediaries in a supply chain: "cutting out the middleman". Instead of going through traditional distribution channels, which had some type of intermediate (such as a distributor, wholesaler, broker, or agent), companies may now deal with every customer directly, for example via the Internet. One important factor is a drop in the cost of servicing customers directly.
Selection	In the context of evolution, certain traits or alleles of a species may be subject to selection. Under selection, individuals with advantageous or "adaptive" traits tend to be more successful than their peers reproductively--meaning they contribute more offspring to the succeeding generation than others do. When these traits have a genetic basis, selection can increase the prevalence of those traits, because offspring will inherit those traits from their parents.
Services marketing	Services marketing is marketing based on relationship and value. It may be used to market a service or a product. Marketing a service-base business is different from marketing a goods-base business.
Partnership	Partnerships may be formed in the legal forms of General Partnership (Offene Handelsgesellschaft, OHG) or Limited Partnership (Kommanditgesellschaft, KG). A Partnership can be formed by only one person. In the OHG, all partners are fully liable for the Partnership"s debts, whereas in the KG there are general partners with unlimited liability and limited partners whose liability is restricted to their fixed contributions to the Partnership.

Business-to-business	Business-to-business (B2B) describes commerce transactions between businesses, such as between a manufacturer and a wholesaler) and business-to-government (B2G).
	The volume of B2B transactions is much higher than the volume of B2C transactions.
Data migration	Data migration is the process of transferring data between storage types, formats, freeing up human resources from tedious tasks. It is required when organizations or individuals change computer systems or upgrade to new systems, or when systems merge (such as when the organizations that use them undergo a merger/takeover).
Internet marketing	Internet marketing, also referred to as i-marketing, web marketing, online marketing, is the marketing of products, or, services over the Internet.
	The Internet has brought media to a global audience. The interactive nature of Internet marketing, both, in terms of providing instant response and eliciting responses, is a unique quality of the medium.
Solution	In chemistry, a solution is a homogeneous mixture composed of two or more substances. In such a mixture, a solute is dissolved in another substance, known as a solvent. Gases may dissolve in liquids, for example, carbon dioxide or oxygen in water.
Strategy	A Strategy is a plan of action designed to achieve a particular goal.
	Strategy is different from tactics. In military terms, tactics is concerned with the conduct of an engagement while Strategy is concerned with how different engagements are linked.
Restrictive	In semantics, a modifier is said to be restrictive (or defining) if it restricts the reference of its head. For example, in "the red car is fancier than the blue one", red and blue are restrictive, because they restrict which cars car and one are referring to. ("The car is fancier than the one" would make little sense).
Intranet	An Intranet is a private computer network that uses Internet Protocol technologies to securely share any part of an organization"s information or operational systems within that organization. The term is used in contrast to internet, a network between organizations, and instead refers to a network within an organization. Sometimes the term refers only to the organization"s internal website, but may be a more extensive part of the organization"s information technology infrastructure.
Extranet	An Extranet is a private network that uses Internet protocols, network connectivity, and possibly the public telecommunication system to securely share part of an organization"s information or operations with suppliers, vendors, partners, customers or other businesses. An Extranet can be viewed as part of a company"s intranet that is extended to users outside the company, usually via the Internet. It has also been described as a "state of mind" in which the Internet is perceived as a way to do business with a selected set of other companies (business-to-business, B2B), in isolation from all other Internet users.
Stereotype	A stereotype is a commonly held public belief about specific social groups, based on some prior assumptions.

Ryder	Ryder System, Inc. (NYSE: R) is an American-based provider of transportation and supply chain management solutions with global operations. Ryder specializes in fleet management, supply chain management and dedicated contracted carriage.
Truck	A Truck or lorry is a motor vehicle - more specifically a commercial vehicle commonly used for transporting goods and materials. Some light Trucks/lorries are similar in size to a passenger automobile. Commercial transportation Trucks/lorries or fire Trucks can be large, and can also serve as a platform for specialized equipment.
Role	A role or a social role is a set of connected behaviors, rights and obligations as conceptualized by actors in a social situation. It is an expected behavior in a given individual social status and social position. It is vital to both functionalist and interactionist understandings of society.
Technology	Technology is a broad concept that deals with an animal species" usage and knowledge of tools and crafts, and how it affects an animal species" ability to control and adapt to its environment. Technology is a term with origins in the Greek "technologia", "τεχνολογÎ¯α" -- "techne", "τÎ¯χνη" and "logia", "λογÎ¯α" ("saying".) However, a strict definition is elusive; "Technology" can refer to material objects of use to humanity, such as machines, hardware or utensils, but can also encompass broader themes, including systems, methods of organization, and techniques.
Transaction cost	In economics and related disciplines, a Transaction cost is a cost incurred in making an economic exchange (restated: the cost of participating in a market.) For example, most people, when buying or selling a stock, must pay a commission to their broker; that commission is a Transaction cost of doing the stock deal. Or consider buying a banana from a store; to purchase the banana, your costs will be not only the price of the banana itself, but also the energy and effort it requires to find out which of the various banana products you prefer, where to get them and at what price, the cost of traveling from your house to the store and back, the time waiting in line, and the effort of the paying itself; the costs above and beyond the cost of the banana are the Transaction cost s.
International finance	International finance is the branch of economics that studies the dynamics of exchange rates, foreign investment, and how these affect international trade. It also studies international projects, international investments and capital flows, and trade deficits. It includes the study of futures, options and currency swaps.
Supply chain	A Supply chain or logistics network is the system of organizations, people, technology, activities, information and resources involved in moving a product or service from supplier to customer. Supply chain activities transform natural resources, raw materials and components into a finished product that is delivered to the end customer. In sophisticated Supply chain systems, used products may re-enter the Supply chain at any point where residual value is recyclable.
Dangerous goods	Dangerous goods,), are solids, liquids, other living organisms, property, or the environment. They are often subject to chemical regulations. dangerous goods include materials that are radioactive, flammable, explosive or corrosive, oxidizers or asphyxiants, biohazardous, toxic, pathogen or allergen substances and organisms.

Note	In music, the term Note has two primary meanings: · a sign used in musical notation to represent the relative duration and pitch of a sound; · a pitched sound itself. Notes are the "atoms" of much Western music: discretizations of musical phenomena that facilitate performance, comprehension, and analysis . The term "Note" can be used in both generic and specific senses: one might say either "the piece Happy Birthday to You begins with two Notes having the same pitch," or "the piece begins with two repetitions of the same Note." In the former case, one uses "Note" to refer to a specific musical event; in the latter, one uses the term to refer to a class of events sharing the same pitch.
Consumer	Consumer is a broad label for any individuals or households that use goods and services generated within the economy. The concept of a Consumer is used in different contexts, so that the usage and significance of the term may vary. Typically when business people and economists talk of Consumers they are talking about person as Consumer, an aggregated commodity item with little individuality other than that expressed in the buy/not-buy decision.
Reverse auction	A Reverse auction is a tool used in industrial business-to-business procurement. It is a type of auction in which the role of the buyer and seller are reversed, with the primary objective to drive purchase prices downward. In an ordinary auction, buyers compete to obtain a good or service.
Business marketing	Business marketing is the practice of individuals, or organizations, including commercial businesses, governments and institutions, facilitating the sale of their products or services to other companies or organizations that in turn resell them, use them as components in products or services they offer or use them to support their operations. Also known as industrial marketing, Business marketing is also called business-to-Business marketing, or B2B marketing, for short. (Note that while marketing to government entities shares some of the same dynamics of organizational marketing, B2G Marketing is meaningfully different).
Disintermediation	In economics, Disintermediation is the removal of intermediaries in a supply chain: "cutting out the middleman". Instead of going through traditional distribution channels, which had some type of intermediate (such as a distributor, wholesaler, broker, or agent), companies may now deal with every customer directly, for example via the Internet. One important factor is a drop in the cost of servicing customers directly.
Consideration	Consideration is the legal concept of value in connection with contracts. It is anything of value in the common sense, promised to another when making a contract. It can take the form of money, physical objects, services, promised actions, or even abstinence from a future action.

Pricing	Pricing is a fundamental aspect of financial modelling, and is one of the four Ps of the marketing mix. The other three aspects are product, promotion, and place. It is also a key variable in microeconomic price allocation theory.
Promotion	Promotion involves disseminating information about a product, product line, brand, or company. It is one of the four key aspects of the marketing mix. (The other three elements are product marketing, pricing, and distribution). P>Promotion is generally sub-divided into two parts: · Above the line Promotion: Promotion in the media (e.g. TV, radio, newspapers, Internet and Mobile Phones) in which the advertiser pays an advertising agency to place the ad · Below the line Promotion: All other Promotion. Much of this is intended to be subtle enough for the consumer to be unaware that Promotion is taking place. E.g. sponsorship, product placement, endorsements, sales Promotion, merchandising, direct mail, personal selling, public relations, trade shows
Sale	A sale is the pinnacle activity involved in selling products or services in return for money or other compensation. It is an act of completion of a commercial activity. A sale is completed by the seller, the owner of the goods.
Case study	A case study is one of several ways of doing research whether it is social science related or even socially related. It is an intensive study of a single group, incident, or community. Other ways include experiments, surveys, or analysis of archival information .

118

Supply chain	A Supply chain or logistics network is the system of organizations, people, technology, activities, information and resources involved in moving a product or service from supplier to customer. Supply chain activities transform natural resources, raw materials and components into a finished product that is delivered to the end customer. In sophisticated Supply chain systems, used products may re-enter the Supply chain at any point where residual value is recyclable.
Partnership	Partnerships may be formed in the legal forms of General Partnership (Offene Handelsgesellschaft, OHG) or Limited Partnership (Kommanditgesellschaft, KG). A Partnership can be formed by only one person. In the OHG, all partners are fully liable for the Partnership"s debts, whereas in the KG there are general partners with unlimited liability and limited partners whose liability is restricted to their fixed contributions to the Partnership.
Internet marketing	Internet marketing, also referred to as i-marketing, web marketing, online marketing, is the marketing of products, or, services over the Internet. The Internet has brought media to a global audience. The interactive nature of Internet marketing, both, in terms of providing instant response and eliciting responses, is a unique quality of the medium.
Procurement	Procurement is the acquisition of goods and/or services at the best possible total cost of ownership, in the right quality and quantity, at the right time, in the right place and from the right source for the direct benefit or use of corporations, individuals, generally via a contract, or it can be the same way selection for human resource Simple Procurement may involve nothing more than repeat purchasing. Complex Procurement could involve finding long term partners - or even "co-destiny" suppliers that might fundamentally commit one organization to another. Almost all purchasing decisions include factors such as delivery and handling, marginal benefit, and price fluctuations.
Time	Time is a component of the measuring system used to sequence events, to compare the durations of events and the intervals between them, and to quantify the motions of objects. time has been a major subject of religion, philosophy, and science, but defining time in a non-controversial manner applicable to all fields of study has consistently eluded the greatest scholars. In physics and other sciences, time is considered one of the few fundamental quantities.
Time-space compression	Time-space compression is a term used to describe processes that seem to accelerate the experience of time and reduce the significance of distance during a given historical moment. Geographer David Harvey used the term in The Condition of Postmodernity, where it refers to "processes that .
Waste minimisation	Waste hierarchy Waste minimisation is the process and the policy of reducing the amount of waste produced by a person or a society. Waste minimisation involves efforts to minimise resource and energy use during manufacture. For the same commercial output, usually the fewer materials are used, the less waste is produced.

Goal

A Goal or objective is a projected state of affairs that a person or a system plans or intends to achieve--a personal or organizational desired end-point in some sort of assumed development. Many people endeavor to reach Goals within a finite time by setting deadlines.

A desire or an intention becomes a Goal if and only if one activates an action for achieving it .

Technology

Technology is a broad concept that deals with an animal species" usage and knowledge of tools and crafts, and how it affects an animal species" ability to control and adapt to its environment. Technology is a term with origins in the Greek "technologia", "τεχνολογîÂ¯α" -- "techne", "τîÂχνη" and "logia", "λογîÂ¯α" ("saying".) However, a strict definition is elusive; "Technology" can refer to material objects of use to humanity, such as machines, hardware or utensils, but can also encompass broader themes, including systems, methods of organization, and techniques.

File sharing

File sharing is the practice of distributing or providing access to digitally stored information, such as computer programs, multi-media (audio, video), documents, transmission, and distribution models. Common methods are manual sharing using removable media, centralized computer file server installations on computer networks, World Wide Web-based hyperlinked documents, and the use of distributed peer-to-peer (P2P) networking.

Toyota

Toyota Motor Corporation is a multinational corporation headquartered in Japan, and currently the world"s largest automaker. Toyota employs approximately 316,000 people around the world.

In 1934, while still a department of Toyota Industries, it created its first product Type A engine and in 1936 its first passenger car the Toyota AA.

Supplier

A supply chain is the system of organizations, people, technology, activities, information and resources involved in moving a product or service from Supplier to customer. Supply chain activities transform natural resources, raw materials and components into a finished product that is delivered to the end customer. In sophisticated supply chain systems, used products may re-enter the supply chain at any point where residual value is recyclable.

Logistics

Logistics is the management of the flow of goods, information and other resources, including energy and people, between the point of origin and the point of consumption in order to meet the requirements of consumers (frequently, and originally, military organizations). Logistics involves the integration of information, transportation, inventory, warehousing, material-handling, and packaging, and occasionally security. Logistics is a channel of the supply chain which adds the value of time and place utility.

Flow network

In graph theory, a flow network is a directed graph where each edge has a capacity and each edge receives a flow. The amount of flow on an edge cannot exceed the capacity of the edge. Often in Operations Research, a directed graph is called a network, the vertices are called nodes and the edges are called arcs.

Inventory	Inventory is a list for goods and materials, held available in stock by a business. It is also used for a list of the contents of a household and for a list for testamentary purposes of the possessions of someone who has died. In accounting Inventory is considered an asset.
Just-in-time	Just in Time could refer to the following: · Just-in-time (business), an inventory strategy that reduces in-process inventory · Just-in-time compilation, a technique for improving the performance of bytecode-compiled programming systems · "Just in Time," a 1956 popular song composed by Jule Styne with lyrics written by Betty Comden and Adolph Green, best known in a recording by Tony Bennett · Just in Time (film), a 2006 British film "
Marketing	marketing is a "social and managerial process by which individuals and groups obtain what they need and want through creating and exchanging products and values with others." It is an integrated process through which companies create value for customers and build strong customer relationships in order to capture value from customers in return. marketing is used to create the customer, to keep the customer and to satisfy the customer. With the customer as the focus of its activities, it can be concluded that marketing management is one of the major components of business management.
Role	A role or a social role is a set of connected behaviors, rights and obligations as conceptualized by actors in a social situation. It is an expected behavior in a given individual social status and social position. It is vital to both functionalist and interactionist understandings of society.
Sale	A sale is the pinnacle activity involved in selling products or services in return for money or other compensation. It is an act of completion of a commercial activity. A sale is completed by the seller, the owner of the goods.
Total cost	In economics, and cost accounting, Total cost describes the total economic cost of production and is made up of variable costs, which vary according to the quantity of a good produced and include inputs such as labor and raw materials, plus fixed costs, which are independent of the quantity of a good produced and include inputs (capital) that cannot be varied in the short term, such as buildings and machinery. Total cost in economics includes the total opportunity cost of each factor of production in addition to fixed and variable costs. The rate at which Total cost changes as the amount produced changes is called marginal cost.
Activity-based costing	Activity-based costing (ABC) is a costing model that identifies activities in an organization and assigns the cost of each activity resource to all products and services according to the actual consumption by each: it assigns more indirect costs (overhead) into direct costs. In this way an organization can precisely estimate the cost of its individual products and services for the purposes of identifying and eliminating those which are unprofitable and lowering the prices of those which are overpriced.

	In a business organization, the ABC methodology assigns an organization"s resource costs through activities to the products and services provided to its customers.
Business-to-business	Business-to-business (B2B) describes commerce transactions between businesses, such as between a manufacturer and a wholesaler) and business-to-government (B2G).
	The volume of B2B transactions is much higher than the volume of B2C transactions.
Total cost of ownership	Total cost of ownership is a financial estimate designed to help consumers and enterprise managers assess direct and indirect costs It is a form of full cost accounting.
Customer profitability	Customer profitability is the difference between the revenues earned from and the costs associated with the customer relationship in a specified period.
	According to Philip Kotler,"a profitable customer is a person, household or a company that overtime, yields a revenue stream that exceeds by an acceptable amount the company"s cost stream of attracting, selling and servicing the customer"
	Although Customer profitability is nothing more than the result of applying the business concept of profit to a customer relationship, measuring the profitability of a firm"s customers or customer groups can often deliver useful business insights.
	Quite often a very small percentage of the firm"s best customers will account for a large portion of firm profit.
Dangerous goods	Dangerous goods,), are solids, liquids, other living organisms, property, or the environment. They are often subject to chemical regulations. dangerous goods include materials that are radioactive, flammable, explosive or corrosive, oxidizers or asphyxiants, biohazardous, toxic, pathogen or allergen substances and organisms.
Transportation	Transport or Transportation is the movement of people and goods from one location to another. Transport is performed by various modes, such as air, rail, road, water, cable, pipeline and space. The field can be divided into infrastructure, vehicles, and operations.
Outsourcing	Outsourcing is subcontracting a service, such as product design or manufacturing, to a third-party company. The decision whether to outsource or to do inhouse is often based upon achieving a lower production cost, making better use of available resources, focussing energy on the core competencies of a particular business, or just making more efficient use of labor, capital, information technology or land resources. It is essentially a division of labour.
Speed	Speed is the rate of motion, or equivalently the rate of change of distance.
	speed is a scalar quantity with dimensions length/time; the equivalent vector quantity to speed is velocity. speed is measured in the same physical units of measurement as velocity, but does not contain the element of direction that velocity has.

Quality	Quality in business, engineering and manufacturing has a pragmatic interpretation as the non-inferiority or superiority of something. Quality is a perceptual, conditional and somewhat subjective attribute and may be understood differently by different people. Consumers may focus on the specification Quality of a product/service, or how it compares to competitors in the marketplace.
Total Quality Management	Total Quality Management is a business management strategy aimed at embedding awareness of quality in all organizational processes. Total Quality Management has been widely used in manufacturing, education, call centers, government, and service industries, as well as NASA space and science programs.

When used together as a phrase, the three words in this expression have the following meanings:

· Total: Involving the entire organization, supply chain, and/or product life cycle
· Quality: With its usual definitions, with all its complexities
· Management: The system of managing with steps like Plan, Organize, Control, Lead, Staff, provisioning and organizing.

As defined by the International Organization for Standardization (ISO):

"Total Quality Management is a management approach for an organization, centered on quality, based on the participation of all its members and aiming at long-term success through customer satisfaction, and benefits to all members of the organization and to society." ISO 8402:1994

One major aim is to reduce variation from every process so that greater consistency of effort is obtained. (Royse, D., Thyer, B., Padgett D., ' Logan T., 2006)

In Japan, Total Quality Management comprises four process steps, namely:

· Kaizen - Focuses on "Continuous Process Improvement", to make processes visible, repeatable and measurable.
· Atarimae Hinshitsu - The idea that "things will work as they are supposed to" .
· Kansei - Examining the way the user applies the product leads to improvement in the product itself.
· Miryokuteki Hinshitsu - The idea that "things should have an aesthetic quality" (for example, a pen will write in a way that is pleasing to the writer.)

Total Quality Management requires that the company maintain this quality standard in all aspects of its business. This requires ensuring that things are done right the first time and that defects and waste are eliminated from operations.

Third-party logistics	A Third-party logistics provider is a firm that provides a one stop shop service to its customers of outsourced (or "third party") logistics services for part, warehousing and transportation services that can be scaled and customized to customer"s needs based on market conditions and the demands and delivery service requirements for their products and materials.

To put forward some standard definitions, we would adopt the definition of 3PL found in the Council of Supply Chain Management Professionals" glossary, which reads as follows:

"A firm [that] provides multiple logistics services for use by customers.

Global strategy

Global strategy as defined in business terms is an organization"s strategic guide to globalization. A sound global strategy should address these questions: what must be (versus what is) the extent of market presence in the world"s major markets? How to build the necessary global presence? What must be (versus what is) the optimal locations around the world for the various value chain activities? How to run global presence into global competitive advantage?

Academic research on global strategy came of age during the 1980s, including work by Michael Porter and Christopher Bartlett ' Sumantra Ghoshal. Among the forces perceived to bring about the globalization of competition were convergence in economic systems and technological change, especially in information technology, that facilitated and required the coordination of a multinational firm"s strategy on a worldwide scale.

Pricing	Pricing is a fundamental aspect of financial modelling, and is one of the four Ps of the marketing mix. The other three aspects are product, promotion, and place. It is also a key variable in microeconomic price allocation theory.
Strategy	A Strategy is a plan of action designed to achieve a particular goal. Strategy is different from tactics. In military terms, tactics is concerned with the conduct of an engagement while Strategy is concerned with how different engagements are linked.
Value	A personal and cultural value is a relative ethic value, an assumption upon which implementation can be extrapolated. A value system is a set of consistent values and measures that is soo not true. A principle value is a foundation upon which other values and measures of integrity are based.
Case study	A case study is one of several ways of doing research whether it is social science related or even socially related. It is an intensive study of a single group, incident, or community. Other ways include experiments, surveys, or analysis of archival information .
Balanced scorecard	The Balanced scorecard (BSC) is a strategic performance management tool for measuring whether the smaller-scale operational activities of a company are aligned with its larger-scale objectives in terms of vision and strategy. By focusing not only on financial outcomes but also on the operational, marketing and developmental inputs to these, the Balanced scorecard helps provide a more comprehensive view of a business, which in turn helps organizations act in their best long-term interests. This tool is also being used to address business response to climate change and greenhouse gas emissions.
Total cost	In economics, and cost accounting, Total cost describes the total economic cost of production and is made up of variable costs, which vary according to the quantity of a good produced and include inputs such as labor and raw materials, plus fixed costs, which are independent of the quantity of a good produced and include inputs (capital) that cannot be varied in the short term, such as buildings and machinery. Total cost in economics includes the total opportunity cost of each factor of production in addition to fixed and variable costs. The rate at which Total cost changes as the amount produced changes is called marginal cost.
Value-based pricing	Value-based pricing, or Value optimized pricing is a business strategy. It sets selling prices on the perceived value to the customer, rather than on the actual cost of the product, the market price, competitors prices, or the historical price. The goal of Value-based pricing is to align price with value delivered.
Product	When a product reaches the maturity stage of the product life cycle a company may choose to operate strategies to extend the life of the product. If the product is predicted to continue to be successful or an upgrade is soon to be released the company can use various methods to keep sales, else the product will be left as is to continue to the decline stage. Examples of extension strategies are:

· Discounted price

· Increased advertising

· Accessing another market abroad

Another strategy is added value.

This is a widely used extension strategy.

Economic value	The economic value of a good or service has puzzled economists since the beginning of the discipline. First, economists tried to estimate the value of a good to an individual alone, and extend that definition to goods which can be exchanged. From this analysis came the concepts value in use and value in exchange.
Determinant	In algebra, the determinant is a special number associated to any square matrix, that is to say, a rectangular array of numbers where the (finite) number of rows and columns are equal. The fundamental geometric meaning of a determinant is a scale factor for measure when the matrix is regarded as a linear transformation. Thus a 2×2 matrix with determinant 2 when applied to a set of points with finite area will transform those points into a set with twice the area.
Commodity	A Commodity is some good for which there is demand, but which is supplied without qualitative differentiation across a market. It is a product that is the same no matter who produces it, such as petroleum, notebook paper, or milk. In other words, copper is copper.
The demand	Perfectly inelastic demand Perfectly elastic demand A price fall usually results in an increase in the quantity demanded by consumers . The demand for a good is relatively inelastic when the change in quantity demanded is less than change in price. Goods and services for which no substitutes exist are generally inelastic.
Customer satisfaction	Customer satisfaction, a business term, is a measure of how products and services supplied by a company meet or surpass customer expectation. It is seen as a key performance indicator within business and is part of the four perspectives of a Balanced Scorecard. In a competitive marketplace where businesses compete for customers, Customer satisfaction is seen as a key differentiator and increasingly has become a key element of business strategy.
Switching cost	Switching barriers or Switching cost s are terms used in microeconomics, strategic management, and marketing to describe any impediment to a customer"s changing of suppliers. In many markets, consumers are forced to incur costs when switching from one supplier to another. These costs are called Switching cost s and can come in many different shapes.
Target costing	Target costing is a pricing method used by firms. It is defined as "a cost management tool for reducing the overall cost of a product over its entire life-cycle with the help of production, engineering, research and design". Target costing finds the maximum amount of cost that can be incurred on a product and with it the firm can still earn the required profit margin from that product at a particular selling price.

Competition	Co-operative competition is based upon promoting mutual survival - "everyone wins". Adam Smith"s "invisible hand" is a process where individuals compete to improve their level of happiness but compete in a cooperative manner through peaceful exchange and without violating other people. Cooperative competition focuses individuals/groups/organisms against the environment.
Product life cycle	Product life cycle Management is the succession of strategies used by management as a product goes through its product life cycle. The conditions in which a product is sold changes over time and must be managed as it moves through its succession of stages. The product life cycle goes through many phases, involves many professional disciplines, and requires many skills, tools and processes.
Time	Time is a component of the measuring system used to sequence events, to compare the durations of events and the intervals between them, and to quantify the motions of objects. time has been a major subject of religion, philosophy, and science, but defining time in a non-controversial manner applicable to all fields of study has consistently eluded the greatest scholars. In physics and other sciences, time is considered one of the few fundamental quantities.
Product line	There are many important decisions about product and service development and marketing. In the process of product development and marketing we should focus on strategic decisions about product attributes, product branding, product packaging, product labeling and product support services. But product strategy also calls for building a Product line.
Robinson-Patman Act	The Robinson-Patman Act of 1936 (or Anti-Price Discrimination Act, 15 U.S.C. § 13) is a United States federal law that prohibits what were considered, at the time of passage, to be anticompetitive practices by producers, specifically price discrimination. It grew out of practices in which chain stores were allowed to purchase goods at lower prices than other retailers.
Consideration	Consideration is the legal concept of value in connection with contracts. It is anything of value in the common sense, promised to another when making a contract. It can take the form of money, physical objects, services, promised actions, or even abstinence from a future action.
Co-operative competition	Co-operative competition is based upon promoting mutual survival - "everyone wins". Adam Smith"s "invisible hand" is a process where individuals compete to improve their level of happiness but compete in a cooperative manner through peaceful exchange and without violating other people. Cooperative competition focuses individuals/groups/organisms against the environment.
Competitive	Competitiveness is a comparative concept of the ability and performance of a firm, sub-sector or country to sell and supply goods and/or services in a given market. Although widely used in economics and business management, the usefulness of the concept, particularly in the context of national competitiveness, is vigorously disputed by economists, such as Paul Krugman . The term may also be applied to markets, where it is used to refer to the extent to which the market structure may be regarded as perfectly competitive.

Procurement	Procurement is the acquisition of goods and/or services at the best possible total cost of ownership, in the right quality and quantity, at the right time, in the right place and from the right source for the direct benefit or use of corporations, individuals, generally via a contract, or it can be the same way selection for human resource Simple Procurement may involve nothing more than repeat purchasing. Complex Procurement could involve finding long term partners - or even "co-destiny" suppliers that might fundamentally commit one organization to another. Almost all purchasing decisions include factors such as delivery and handling, marginal benefit, and price fluctuations.
Reverse auction	A Reverse auction is a tool used in industrial business-to-business procurement. It is a type of auction in which the role of the buyer and seller are reversed, with the primary objective to drive purchase prices downward. In an ordinary auction, buyers compete to obtain a good or service.

138

Chapter 15. Advertising and Sales Promotion

Celebrity branding	Celebrity branding is a type of branding, in which a celebrity uses his or her status in society to promote a product, service or charity. Celebrity branding can take several different forms, from a celebrity simply appearing in advertisements for a product, service or charity, to a celebrity attending PR events, creating his or her own line of products or services, and/or using his or her name as a brand. The most popular forms of celebrity brand lines are for clothing and fragrances.
Business marketing	Business marketing is the practice of individuals, or organizations, including commercial businesses, governments and institutions, facilitating the sale of their products or services to other companies or organizations that in turn resell them, use them as components in products or services they offer or use them to support their operations. Also known as industrial marketing, Business marketing is also called business-to-Business marketing, or B2B marketing, for short. (Note that while marketing to government entities shares some of the same dynamics of organizational marketing, B2G Marketing is meaningfully different).
Marketing communication	Marketing communications (or MarCom or Integrated marketing communications) are messages and related media used to communicate with a market. Those who practice advertising, branding, direct marketing, graphic design, marketing, packaging, promotion, publicity, sponsorship, public relations, sales, sales promotion and online marketing are termed marketing communicators, marketing communication managers, or more briefly as marcom managers.
	Traditionally, marketing communication practitioners focus on the creation and execution of printed marketing collateral; however, academic and professional research developed the practice to use strategic elements of branding and marketing in order to ensure consistency of message delivery throughout an organization - the same "look ' feel".
Search engine marketing	Search engine marketing is a form of Internet marketing that seeks to promote websites by increasing their visibility in search engine result pages (SERPs.) According to the Search engine marketing Professional Organization, Search engine marketing methods include: search engine optimization (or SEO), paid placement, contextual advertising, and paid inclusion. Other sources, including the New York Times, define Search engine marketing as the practice of buying paid search listings.
Case study	A case study is one of several ways of doing research whether it is social science related or even socially related. It is an intensive study of a single group, incident, or community. Other ways include experiments, surveys, or analysis of archival information .
Role	A role or a social role is a set of connected behaviors, rights and obligations as conceptualized by actors in a social situation. It is an expected behavior in a given individual social status and social position. It is vital to both functionalist and interactionist understandings of society.
Strategy	A Strategy is a plan of action designed to achieve a particular goal.
	Strategy is different from tactics. In military terms, tactics is concerned with the conduct of an engagement while Strategy is concerned with how different engagements are linked.

141

Interactive marketing	Interactive marketing refers to the evolving trend in marketing whereby marketing has moved from a transaction-based effort to a conversation. The definition of Interactive marketing comes from John Deighton at Harvard, who says Interactive marketing is the ability to address the customer, remember what the customer says and address the customer again in a way that illustrates that we remember what the customer has told us (Deighton 1996). Interactive marketing is not synonymous with online marketing, although Interactive marketing processes are facilitated by internet technology.
Business-to-business	Business-to-business (B2B) describes commerce transactions between businesses, such as between a manufacturer and a wholesaler) and business-to-government (B2G). The volume of B2B transactions is much higher than the volume of B2C transactions.
Restrictive	In semantics, a modifier is said to be restrictive (or defining) if it restricts the reference of its head. For example, in "the red car is fancier than the blue one", red and blue are restrictive, because they restrict which cars car and one are referring to. ("The car is fancier than the one" would make little sense).
Target audience	In marketing and advertising, a target audience usually an advertising campaign, is aimed at appealing to. A target audience can be people of a certain age group, gender, marital status, etc. (ex: teenagers, females, single people, etc.)
Dangerous goods	Dangerous goods,), are solids, liquids, other living organisms, property, or the environment. They are often subject to chemical regulations. dangerous goods include materials that are radioactive, flammable, explosive or corrosive, oxidizers or asphyxiants, biohazardous, toxic, pathogen or allergen substances and organisms.
Selection	In the context of evolution, certain traits or alleles of a species may be subject to selection. Under selection, individuals with advantageous or "adaptive" traits tend to be more successful than their peers reproductively--meaning they contribute more offspring to the succeeding generation than others do. When these traits have a genetic basis, selection can increase the prevalence of those traits, because offspring will inherit those traits from their parents.
Original equipment manufacturer	An Original equipment manufacturer, manufactures products or components which are purchased by a second company and retailed under the second company"s brand name. It is a form of outsourcing. When referring to automotive parts, Original equipment manufacturer designates a replacement part made by the manufacturer of the original part.
Publication	The word publication means the act of publishing, and it also means any writing of which copies are published, and any website. Among publication s are books, and periodicals, the latter including magazines, scholarly journals, and newspapers. publication is a technical term in legal contexts and especially important in copyright legislation.
Direct marketing	Direct marketing is a sub-discipline and type of marketing. There are two main definitional characteristics which distinguish it from other types of marketing. The first is that it attempts to send its messages directly to consumers, without the use of intervening media.

E-mail marketing	E-mail marketing is a form of direct marketing which uses electronic mail as a means of communicating commercial or fundraising messages to an audience. In its broadest sense, every e-mail sent to a potential or current customer could be considered E-mail marketing. However, the term is usually used to refer to: · sending e-mails with the purpose of enhancing the relationship of a merchant with its current or previous customers and to encourage customer loyalty and repeat business, · sending e-mails with the purpose of acquiring new customers or convincing current customers to purchase something immediately, · adding advertisements to e-mails sent by other companies to their customers, and · sending e-mails over the Internet, as e-mail did and does exist outside the Internet (e.g., network e-mail and FIDO). Researchers estimate that United States firms alone spent US$400 million on E-mail marketing in 2006.
Sale	A sale is the pinnacle activity involved in selling products or services in return for money or other compensation. It is an act of completion of a commercial activity. A sale is completed by the seller, the owner of the goods.
Accounting profit	Accounting profit is the difference between price and the costs of bringing to market whatever it is that is accounted as an enterprise (whether by harvest, extraction, manufacture) in terms of the component costs of delivered goods and/or services and any operating or other expenses. A key difficulty in measuring profit is in defining costs. Pure economic monetary profits can be zero or negative even in competitive equilibrium when accounted monetized costs exceed monetized price.
Mind control	Mind control (also referred to as brainwashing, coercive persuasion, and thought reform) refers to a broad range of psychological tactics thought to subvert an individual"s control of his or her own thinking, behavior, emotions).
Trade	Trade is the voluntary exchange of goods, services, or both. trade is also called commerce. A mechanism that allows trade is called a market.
Efficiency	In statistics, efficiency is a term used in the comparison of various statistical procedures and, in particular, it refers to a measure of the desirability of an estimator or of an experimental design. The relative efficiency of two procedures is the ratio their efficiencies, although often this term is used where the comparison is made between a given procedure and a notional "best possible" procedure. The efficiencies and the relative efficiency of two procedures theoretically depend on the sample size available for the given procedure, but it is often possible to use the asymptotic relative efficiency (defined as the limit of the relative efficiencies as the sample size grows) as the principal comparison measure.

Business marketing	Business marketing is the practice of individuals, or organizations, including commercial businesses, governments and institutions, facilitating the sale of their products or services to other companies or organizations that in turn resell them, use them as components in products or services they offer or use them to support their operations. Also known as industrial marketing, Business marketing is also called business-to-Business marketing, or B2B marketing, for short. (Note that while marketing to government entities shares some of the same dynamics of organizational marketing, B2G Marketing is meaningfully different).
Personal	A personal ad is an item or notice traditionally in the newspaper, similar to a classified ad but personal in nature. In British English it is also commonly known as an advert in a lonely hearts column. With its rise in popularity, the World Wide Web has also become a common medium for personals, commonly referred to as online dating.
Celebrity branding	Celebrity branding is a type of branding, in which a celebrity uses his or her status in society to promote a product, service or charity. Celebrity branding can take several different forms, from a celebrity simply appearing in advertisements for a product, service or charity, to a celebrity attending PR events, creating his or her own line of products or services, and/or using his or her name as a brand. The most popular forms of celebrity brand lines are for clothing and fragrances.
Marketing communication	Marketing communications (or MarCom or Integrated marketing communications) are messages and related media used to communicate with a market. Those who practice advertising, branding, direct marketing, graphic design, marketing, packaging, promotion, publicity, sponsorship, public relations, sales, sales promotion and online marketing are termed marketing communicators, marketing communication managers, or more briefly as marcom managers.
	Traditionally, marketing communication practitioners focus on the creation and execution of printed marketing collateral; however, academic and professional research developed the practice to use strategic elements of branding and marketing in order to ensure consistency of message delivery throughout an organization - the same "look ' feel".
Dangerous goods	Dangerous goods,), are solids, liquids, other living organisms, property, or the environment. They are often subject to chemical regulations. dangerous goods include materials that are radioactive, flammable, explosive or corrosive, oxidizers or asphyxiants, biohazardous, toxic, pathogen or allergen substances and organisms.
Relationship marketing	Relationship marketing is a form of marketing developed from direct response marketing campaigns conducted in the 1970"s and 1980"s which emphasizes customer retention and satisfaction, rather than a dominant focus on "point of sale" transactions.
	relationship marketing differs from other forms of marketing in that it recognizes the long term value to the firm of keeping customers, as opposed to direct or "Intrusion" marketing, which focuses upon acquisition of new clients by targeting majority demographics based upon prospective client lists.

relationship marketing refers to long-term and mutually beneficial arrangement wherein both buyer and seller focus on value enhancement through the certain of more satisfying exchange. This approach attempts to transcend the simple purchase exchange process with customer to make more meaningful and richer contact by providing a more holistic, personalized purchase, and use orn consumption experience to create stronger ties.

Marketing effectiveness	Marketing effectiveness is the quality of how marketers go to market with the goal of optimizing their spending to achieve good results for both the short-term and long-term. It is also related to Marketing ROI and Return on Marketing Investment (ROMI). marketing effectiveness has four dimensions: · Corporate - Each company operates within certain bounds. These are determined by their size, their budget and their ability to make organizational change.
Strategy	A Strategy is a plan of action designed to achieve a particular goal. Strategy is different from tactics. In military terms, tactics is concerned with the conduct of an engagement while Strategy is concerned with how different engagements are linked.
Sale	A sale is the pinnacle activity involved in selling products or services in return for money or other compensation. It is an act of completion of a commercial activity. A sale is completed by the seller, the owner of the goods.
Organizing	Organizing (also spelled organising) is the act of rearranging elements following one or more rules. Anything is commonly considered organized when it looks like everything has a correct order of placement. But it"s only ultimately organized if any element has no difference on time taken to find it.
Product	When a product reaches the maturity stage of the product life cycle a company may choose to operate strategies to extend the life of the product. If the product is predicted to continue to be successful or an upgrade is soon to be released the company can use various methods to keep sales, else the product will be left as is to continue to the decline stage. Examples of extension strategies are: · Discounted price · Increased advertising · Accessing another market abroad Another strategy is added value. This is a widely used extension strategy.
Customer profitability	Customer profitability is the difference between the revenues earned from and the costs associated with the customer relationship in a specified period. According to Philip Kotler,"a profitable customer is a person, household or a company that overtime, yields a revenue stream that exceeds by an acceptable amount the company"s cost stream of attracting, selling and servicing the customer"

Although Customer profitability is nothing more than the result of applying the business concept of profit to a customer relationship, measuring the profitability of a firm"s customers or customer groups can often deliver useful business insights.

Quite often a very small percentage of the firm"s best customers will account for a large portion of firm profit.

Value	A personal and cultural value is a relative ethic value, an assumption upon which implementation can be extrapolated. A value system is a set of consistent values and measures that is soo not true. A principle value is a foundation upon which other values and measures of integrity are based.
Value proposition	In the field of marketing, a customer Value proposition consists of the sum total of benefits which a vendor promises that a customer will receive in return for the customer"s associated payment (or other value-transfer.)

Put simply, the Value proposition is what the customer gets for his money.

Accordingly, a customer can evaluate a company"s value-proposition on two broad dimensions with multiple subsets:

· relative performance: what the customer gets from the vendor relative to a competitor"s offering;
· price: which consists of the payment the customer makes to acquire the product or service; plus the access cost

The vendor-company"s marketing and sales efforts offer a customer Value proposition; the vendor-company"s delivery and customer-service processes then fulfill that value-proposition.

A value-proposition can assist in a firm"s marketing strategy, and may guide a business to target a particular market segment.

Proposition	This article is about the term proposition in logic and philosophy; for other uses see proposition

In logic and philosophy, proposition refers to either (a) the "content" or "meaning" of a meaningful declarative sentence or (b) the pattern of symbols, marks, or sounds that make up a meaningful declarative sentence. Propositions in either case are intended to be truth-bearers, that is, they are either true or false.

The existence of propositions in the former sense, as well as the existence of "meanings", is disputed by some philosophers.

Competitive	Competitiveness is a comparative concept of the ability and performance of a firm, sub-sector or country to sell and supply goods and/or services in a given market. Although widely used in economics and business management, the usefulness of the concept, particularly in the context of national competitiveness, is vigorously disputed by economists, such as Paul Krugman .

The term may also be applied to markets, where it is used to refer to the extent to which the market structure may be regarded as perfectly competitive.

Internality	An internality is a term used in behavioral economics to describe those types of behaviors that impose costs on a person in the long-run that are not taken into account when making decisions in the present. Classical Economics discourages government from creating legislation that targets internalities, because it is assumed that the consumer takes these personal costs into account when paying for the good that causes the internality. For example, cigarettes should be taxed because of the negative consumption externalities that they impose, such as second-hand smoke, not because the smoker harms him or herself by smoking.
Selection	In the context of evolution, certain traits or alleles of a species may be subject to selection. Under selection, individuals with advantageous or "adaptive" traits tend to be more successful than their peers reproductively--meaning they contribute more offspring to the succeeding generation than others do. When these traits have a genetic basis, selection can increase the prevalence of those traits, because offspring will inherit those traits from their parents.
Job satisfaction	Job satisfaction describes how content an individual is with his or her job. The happier people are within their job, the more satisfied they are said to be. job satisfaction is not the same as motivation, although it is clearly linked.
Case study	A case study is one of several ways of doing research whether it is social science related or even socially related. It is an intensive study of a single group, incident, or community. Other ways include experiments, surveys, or analysis of archival information .

Balanced scorecard	The Balanced scorecard (BSC) is a strategic performance management tool for measuring whether the smaller-scale operational activities of a company are aligned with its larger-scale objectives in terms of vision and strategy. By focusing not only on financial outcomes but also on the operational, marketing and developmental inputs to these, the Balanced scorecard helps provide a more comprehensive view of a business, which in turn helps organizations act in their best long-term interests. This tool is also being used to address business response to climate change and greenhouse gas emissions.
Strategy	A Strategy is a plan of action designed to achieve a particular goal. Strategy is different from tactics. In military terms, tactics is concerned with the conduct of an engagement while Strategy is concerned with how different engagements are linked.
Strategy map	A strategy map is a visual representation of the strategy of an organization. It illustrates how the organization plans to achieve its mission and vision by means of a linked chain of continuous improvements. For a commercial business, the strategy map illustrates the long-term game plan or competitive strategy to achieve increased profitability.
Case study	A case study is one of several ways of doing research whether it is social science related or even socially related. It is an intensive study of a single group, incident, or community. Other ways include experiments, surveys, or analysis of archival information .
Business marketing	Business marketing is the practice of individuals, or organizations, including commercial businesses, governments and institutions, facilitating the sale of their products or services to other companies or organizations that in turn resell them, use them as components in products or services they offer or use them to support their operations. Also known as industrial marketing, Business marketing is also called business-to-Business marketing, or B2B marketing, for short. (Note that while marketing to government entities shares some of the same dynamics of organizational marketing, B2G Marketing is meaningfully different).
Marketing	marketing is a "social and managerial process by which individuals and groups obtain what they need and want through creating and exchanging products and values with others." It is an integrated process through which companies create value for customers and build strong customer relationships in order to capture value from customers in return. marketing is used to create the customer, to keep the customer and to satisfy the customer. With the customer as the focus of its activities, it can be concluded that marketing management is one of the major components of business management.
Marketing communication	Marketing communications (or MarCom or Integrated marketing communications) are messages and related media used to communicate with a market. Those who practice advertising, branding, direct marketing, graphic design, marketing, packaging, promotion, publicity, sponsorship, public relations, sales, sales promotion and online marketing are termed marketing communicators, marketing communication managers, or more briefly as marcom managers.

Traditionally, marketing communication practitioners focus on the creation and execution of printed marketing collateral; however, academic and professional research developed the practice to use strategic elements of branding and marketing in order to ensure consistency of message delivery throughout an organization - the same "look ' feel".

Time	Time is a component of the measuring system used to sequence events, to compare the durations of events and the intervals between them, and to quantify the motions of objects. time has been a major subject of religion, philosophy, and science, but defining time in a non-controversial manner applicable to all fields of study has consistently eluded the greatest scholars. In physics and other sciences, time is considered one of the few fundamental quantities.
Restrictive	In semantics, a modifier is said to be restrictive (or defining) if it restricts the reference of its head. For example, in "the red car is fancier than the blue one", red and blue are restrictive, because they restrict which cars car and one are referring to. ("The car is fancier than the one" would make little sense).
Goal	A Goal or objective is a projected state of affairs that a person or a system plans or intends to achieve--a personal or organizational desired end-point in some sort of assumed development. Many people endeavor to reach Goals within a finite time by setting deadlines. A desire or an intention becomes a Goal if and only if one activates an action for achieving it .
Productivity	Productivity in economics refers to metrics and measures of output from production processes, per unit of input. Labor Productivity, for example, is typically measured as a ratio of output per labor-hour, an input. Productivity may be conceived of as a metrics of the technical or engineering efficiency of production.
Proposition	This article is about the term proposition in logic and philosophy; for other uses see proposition In logic and philosophy, proposition refers to either (a) the "content" or "meaning" of a meaningful declarative sentence or (b) the pattern of symbols, marks, or sounds that make up a meaningful declarative sentence. Propositions in either case are intended to be truth-bearers, that is, they are either true or false. The existence of propositions in the former sense, as well as the existence of "meanings", is disputed by some philosophers.
Value	A personal and cultural value is a relative ethic value, an assumption upon which implementation can be extrapolated. A value system is a set of consistent values and measures that is soo not true. A principle value is a foundation upon which other values and measures of integrity are based.
Value proposition	In the field of marketing, a customer Value proposition consists of the sum total of benefits which a vendor promises that a customer will receive in return for the customer"s associated payment (or other value-transfer.) Put simply, the Value proposition is what the customer gets for his money.

Accordingly, a customer can evaluate a company"s value-proposition on two broad dimensions with multiple subsets:

- · relative performance: what the customer gets from the vendor relative to a competitor"s offering;
- · price: which consists of the payment the customer makes to acquire the product or service; plus the access cost

The vendor-company"s marketing and sales efforts offer a customer Value proposition; the vendor-company"s delivery and customer-service processes then fulfill that value-proposition.

A value-proposition can assist in a firm"s marketing strategy, and may guide a business to target a particular market segment.

Internality

An internality is a term used in behavioral economics to describe those types of behaviors that impose costs on a person in the long-run that are not taken into account when making decisions in the present. Classical Economics discourages government from creating legislation that targets internalities, because it is assumed that the consumer takes these personal costs into account when paying for the good that causes the internality. For example, cigarettes should be taxed because of the negative consumption externalities that they impose, such as second-hand smoke, not because the smoker harms him or herself by smoking.

Resources

Human beings are also considered to be Resources because they have the ability to change raw materials into valuable Resources. The term Human Resources can also be defined as the skills, energies, talents, abilities and knowledge that are used for the production of goods or the rendering of services. While taking into account human beings as Resources, the following things have to be kept in mind:

- · The size of the population
- · The capabilities of the individuals in that population

Many Resources cannot be consumed in their original form. They have to be processed in order to change them into more usable commodities.

Marketing performance measurement

Marketing performance measurement and management is a term used by marketing professionals to describe the analysis and improvement of the efficiency and effectiveness of marketing. This is accomplished by focus on the alignment of marketing activities, strategies, and metrics with business goals. It involves the creation a metrics framework to monitor marketing performance, and then develop and utilize marketing dashboards to manage marketing performance.

Audit

The general definition of an Audit is an evaluation of a person, organization, system, process, enterprise, project or product. Audits are performed to ascertain the validity and reliability of information; also to provide an assessment of a system"s internal control. The goal of an Audit is to express an opinion on the person / organization/system (etc) in question, under evaluation based on work done on a test basis.

Sale	A sale is the pinnacle activity involved in selling products or services in return for money or other compensation. It is an act of completion of a commercial activity. A sale is completed by the seller, the owner of the goods.
Defined	In mathematics, Defined and unDefined are used to explain whether or not expressions have meaningful, sensible, and unambiguous values. Whether an expression has a meaningful value depends on the context of the expression. For example the value of $4 - 5$ is unDefined if a positive integer result is required.
Efficiency	In statistics, efficiency is a term used in the comparison of various statistical procedures and, in particular, it refers to a measure of the desirability of an estimator or of an experimental design. The relative efficiency of two procedures is the ratio their efficiencies, although often this term is used where the comparison is made between a given procedure and a notional "best possible" procedure. The efficiencies and the relative efficiency of two procedures theoretically depend on the sample size available for the given procedure, but it is often possible to use the asymptotic relative efficiency (defined as the limit of the relative efficiencies as the sample size grows) as the principal comparison measure.
Activity-based costing	Activity-based costing (ABC) is a costing model that identifies activities in an organization and assigns the cost of each activity resource to all products and services according to the actual consumption by each: it assigns more indirect costs (overhead) into direct costs. In this way an organization can precisely estimate the cost of its individual products and services for the purposes of identifying and eliminating those which are unprofitable and lowering the prices of those which are overpriced. In a business organization, the ABC methodology assigns an organization"s resource costs through activities to the products and services provided to its customers.
Marketing management	Marketing management is a business discipline which is focused on the practical application of marketing techniques and the management of a firm"s marketing resources and activities. Marketing managers are often responsible for influencing the level, timing, and composition of customer demand accepted definition of the term. In part, this is because the role of a marketing manager can vary significantly based on a business" size, corporate culture, and industry context.
Dangerous goods	Dangerous goods,), are solids, liquids, other living organisms, property, or the environment. They are often subject to chemical regulations. dangerous goods include materials that are radioactive, flammable, explosive or corrosive, oxidizers or asphyxiants, biohazardous, toxic, pathogen or allergen substances and organisms.

CPSIA information can be obtained at www.ICGtesting.com
Printed in the USA
270168BV00002B/64/P